Where Are They N
The '80s Era

Special thanks to Stuart Nudelman

Project Manager: Aaron Stang
Assistant Editor: Colgan Bryan
Production Coordinator: Yoni Leviatan
Cover Illustration: Magdi Rodriguez
Text Editor: Nadine DeMarco

CONTENTS

ARTIST INDEX

The '80s Era: Changes
By Dave Rubin

It was not an auspicious beginning for the new decade. Ronald Reagan, the conservative ex-governor of California and former B-movie actor, was elected President November 4, 1980. John Lennon, after finding peace and harmony with Yoko Ono and satisfaction in his solo career, was shot and killed by a deranged fan outside his apartment building in New York City one month later on December 8. Though it had always been a slim chance at best, the hopes of a Beatles reunion were brutally dashed. Music fans longed for a group or style of music that would provide that sense of community so cherished from the '60s. Though not what was expected, or perhaps even wanted, a rallying point for the rock audience was provided August 1, 1981.

That summer Saturday MTV debuted with its first music video, the Buggles' "Video Killed the Radio Star." It would not be long before the irony inherent in the title would become a prophecy. Videos were about looks, style, and fashion, and viewers loved it from the start. Overnight the director became the creative arbiter, rather than the musicians, just as in the movies. Promotional music shorts had been around since the '40s, and many bands, including the Beatles, had occasionally employed them in the '60s to support the release of a new song. Now, however, the music was vying with the visuals for the viewer's attention. As the productions became more and more elaborate, such as Michael Jackson's $500,000 "Thriller" video from 1984, the video itself became the star. Eventually, video awards would be given out just like Oscars and Emmys. Almost immediately rock musicians with the "right look" advanced their careers via regular appearances in the MTV rotation while others languished. Southern rock, as exemplified by the Charlie Daniels Band, .38 Special, and the Marshall Tucker Band began to slip in popularity since the mostly large, beefy guys playing in these groups did not make the cut. Black musicians, as well, were largely absent, evoking protests. Only with the emergence of rap and hip-hop music would this "oversight" be rectified.

Despite the narrow view espoused on MTV, rock music flourished in the '80s era, especially with the ascendancy of heavy metal. Almost single-handedly Eddie Van Halen brought the guitar hero back into the limelight from whence he had been shunned by punk and pop music in the late '70s. Drawing inspiration from Jimi Hendrix, Eric Clapton, and mainly his own uninhibited approach to technique, "Edward the V" took loud electric guitar out of the '60s and into the '80s. Following in his wake were, among others, Def Leppard, Extreme, and Iron Maiden. To their advantage, most metal rockers had the slim, wiry frames and big hair to guarantee their acceptance on MTV.

Classic '70s acts like ZZ Top®, Aerosmith, Heart, Journey, Tom Petty, Fleetwood Mac, and Santana continued making blues and folk-based rock that had always depended on a big lead guitar sound to make a statement. More pop-oriented bands like Blondie, the Cars, and Talking Heads anchored the genre known as new wave while the Ramones continued exploring the raw side of life with their uncompromising brand of punk. In addition, another classification that began in the '70s, known as jazz-rock, spawned more commercial bands like Toto, even as progressive rockers like Rush continued confounding the critics with their legions of fans. Out on the fringe, the blues would enjoy a revival in the talented hands of Stevie Ray Vaughan and Robert Cray, bringing it partly into the mainstream by the end of the decade.

The popularity of so much accessible music gave rise to active and vital club scenes around the world. Huge music festivals that had attracted such enormous numbers in the '60s and '70s, though, were basically a thing of the past by the '80s. One exception was Live Aid in 1985. Actually two concerts, one in Philadelphia and the other in London, the events were simulcast worldwide on TV and raised more than $50 million for famine relief. Performers included Paul McCartney, Eric Clapton, Tina Turner, Mick Jagger, Jimmy Page and Robert Plant, Phil Collins, U2, Madonna, Sting, George Thorogood, and Albert Collins.

Out in the "straight" world President Reagan was going toe to toe with the Soviet Union, declaring them the "evil empire" and helping to bring down the flagship of the Communist universe by engaging them in a deficit-wrecking arms race. Like John F. Kennedy who had boldly predicted man would go to the moon before the end of the '60s, Reagan badgered the Russians to tear down the Berlin Wall in Germany, and in 1989 it tumbled. Meanwhile, his conservative politics had a counterpart in England where the right-wing Prime Minister Margaret Thatcher reigned with austerity.

Fantasy, romantic adventure, horror, and hyperkinetic action films brought the public out to theaters while home video viewing started to gain in popularity. "Saturday Night Live"'s John Belushi and Dan Ackroyd, the Blues Brothers, appeared in the film of the same name, giving needed exposure to legends like John Lee Hooker, Ray Charles, Aretha Franklin, and James Brown. It has since gone on to achieve cult status, but there were other films with hit soundtracks as well, such as The Big Chill and Dirty Dancing. The blockbuster movies of the time included E.T. and several ongoing series: Indiana Jones, Batman, Star Trek, Superman, Friday the 13th, Death Wish, Poltergeist, The Karate Kid, Police Academy, and Rocky. On TV, it was the era of the situation comedy, led by "M*A*S*H," "The Jeffersons," "The Cosby Show," "Cheers," "The Golden Girls," "Taxi," and "Three's Company."

Vice President George Bush was elected to succeed Reagan in 1988, so the Republican administration spilled over into the '90s. The '80s had been a boom time on Wall Street, but the middle class suffered. Eventually the downward-spiraling economy and the sour taste left by the Iran-Contra Affair would convince voters to swing to the left (or at least the center) and put a saxophone-playing, Elvis-loving "good ole boy" from Arkansas in the White House in 1992. Musicians would follow right along to some extent, with roots and acoustic music rising out of the synthesized pop, rap, and hip-hop prevalent in the '90s era.

Where Are They Now?

Aerosmith

Permanent Vacation reached the Top 20 in 1987 and Pump was a hit at #5 in 1989. Big Ones, a greatest-hits collection from 1994 went double-Platinum. The band endured legal hassles and allegations of continued drug abuse during the early '90s. A Little South of Sanity was Aerosmith's last release in 1998.

Blondie

Lead singer Debbie Harry released a solo album, Koo Koo, in 1981. Blondie's last album was The Hunter in 1982, after which time they split up. Harry continued with her solo career until the band reunited in 1998 for a tour and the recording of No Exit in 1999.

Bon Jovi

The band achieved Platinum success with Slippery When Wet (1986) and New Jersey (1988). Jon then released Blaze of Glory as a solo album in 1990. He re-formed the band in 1992 and recorded Keep the Faith. Returning as a solo artist, his last release was Destination Anywhere in 1998.

The Cars

Panorama hit #5 and went Platinum in 1980. Shake It Up also went Platinum in 1981, and the title track produced the first Top 10 single for the group. In the early '80s various members of the band had solo projects. They came back with Heartbeat City in 1984, and it hit #3 while going triple-Platinum and reaching the Top 10 with the single "You Might Think." Again the group members went and produced solo albums. Door to Door from 1987 had the Top 20 single "You Are the Girl," and then the band broke up in 1988. The individual members continued with solo projects, with lead singer Ric Ocasek being the most successful.

Def Leppard

The band experienced serious problems after Pyromania in 1983. Drummer Rick Allen lost an arm as a result of a serious car accident, but he managed to play with one arm and a special drum kit. Hysteria from 1987 produced six Top 20 singles including "Hysteria," "Pour Some Sugar on Me," "Love Bites," "Armageddon It" and "Rocket." Guitarist Steve Clark OD'd in 1991. Adrenalize reached #1 in 1992 as former Whitesnake guitarist Vivian Campbell joined. Their last record was Euphoria in 1999.

Extreme

"Hole Hearted" reached #4 in 1991. Sales fell off in the '90s, but the band continued recording and touring. Running Gag was their last release in 1998.

Heart

Bad Animals contained the #1 single "Alone" in 1987. In 1990 Brigade produced a #2 single with "All I Want to Do Is Make Love to You." The Wilson sisters formed the acoustic group Lovemongers in the early '90s and returned to Heart in 1993. Their last release was The Road Home in 1995.

Billy Idol

Born William Broad, Idol released Whiplash Smile in 1986 and Charmed Life in 1990. His last recording was L.A. Woman in 1993.

INXS

Lead singer Michael Hutchence released the unsuccessful Max Q in 1990 even as the band followed with X, producing the #2 single "Suicide Blonde." They continued to record and perform through the '90s while Hutchence lived the decadent rock 'n' roll lifestyle, but critics and fans considered the group passé. INXS signed with PolyGram Records in 1994 and three years later released Elegantly Wasted, their biggest seller. Hutchence died under bizarre circumstances in a Sydney, Australia hotel room in 1997.

Iron Maiden

Seventh Son from 1988 was their best album since Number of the Beast in 1982. The band would go on to achieve more success in the U.K. than in the U.S. Blayze Bayley replaced lead singer Bruce Dickinson in 1991. Virtual XI was their last record in 1998.

Journey

After Frontiers in 1983, lead singer Steve Perry released his solo album Street Talk in 1984. Journey disbanded in 1986. Perry went into semi-retirement but released For the Love of Strange Medicine in 1994. When it registered disappointing sales, he re-formed Journey in 1996. Their last record was Trial by Fire in 1996.

Robert Palmer

"I Didn't Mean to Turn You On" from Riptide and "Simply Irresistible" from Heavy Nova both peaked at #2. The change in style from sexy glamour boy that followed, however, hurt sales of Don't Explain (1990) and Ridin' High (1992). The latter featured Tin Pan Alley and cabaret standards. Palmer is still active, however, and he released Woke Up Laughing in 1998 and Rhythm & Blues in 1999.

Tom Petty

Petty and the Heartbreakers made the Platinum Hard Promises in 1981, the Top 10 Long After Dark in 1982, and the Top 10 Platinum Southern Accents in 1985. He joined the Traveling Wilburys in 1988 after having released a triple-Platinum solo album, Full Moon Fever, in 1989. In 1991 he reunited with the Heartbreakers. The band under-went changes of personnel and record companies in the early '90s. Petty's next solo venture, Wild Flowers, also went triple-Platinum in 1994. The group reunited once again in 1996. Echo was their last record in 1999.

Poison

Guitarist C. C. Deville was fired in 1991 for substance abuse and replaced by Richie Kotzen. Native Tongue contained the hit single "Stand" in 1993, the same year Kotzen was replaced by Blues Saraceno. DeVille returned in 1996, replacing Saraceno.

The Ramones

Road to Ruin from 1977 had a more pop sound, and the title was prophetic because their fans and critics resisted the change. The Ramones appeared in the movie Rock 'n' Roll High School in 1979 and tried even more commercial material in the early '80s. They returned closer to their original sound with Too Tough to Die in 1984. In 1989 they provided the theme song for Stephen King's film Pet Sematary. They continued touring and recording with some personnel changes until their break-up in 1996. We're Outta Here was their last record in 1997.

Rush

Grace Under Pressure (1984) and Power Windows (1985) were both Platinum albums, and Roll the Bones (1991) and Counterparts (1993) each hit #3. Echo was their last release in 1996.

Carlos Santana

After many incarnations of the band Santana, since the '80s Carlos Santana has functioned as a solo artist with back-up musicians. In 1992 he released Milagro and in 1994 Santana Brothers. The remarkably successful Supernatural (1999), a series of duets with guest artists, produced the hit single "Smooth" and just may prove to be the most successful Santana album ever—capping a 30-year career in rock. Santana remains a highly respected guitarist among his fans and fellow musicians.

Scandal

The band broke up in 1985 as lead singer Patty Smyth (not to be confused with Patti Smith) went after a solo career.

Talking Heads

The band broke up in 1991 after 12 years of quirky, intellectual "art" music. Leader David Byrne went off on a solo career, and the remaining members formed the Tom Tom Club. In 1996 the band re-formed without Byrne. In 1999 all of the original members got together for the fifteenth anniversary edition of their film, Stop Making Sense.

Toto

Isolation from 1984 went Gold. Toto experienced many personnel changes in the next few years, and drummer Jeff Porcaro died in 1992. Their popularity dropped in the U.S. but maintained in Japan. The band continues to perform and record. Their last recording was Mindfields in 1999.

Van Halen

The premier metal band from the '80s has a history of lead singers leaving due to their conflicts with Eddie. Sammy Hagar replaced original front man David Lee Roth in 1985. Hagar was then replaced briefly by Roth in the mid-'90s. Former Extreme lead singer Gary Cherone then replaced Roth. Eddie played on Michael Jackson's "Beat It" in 1983. Roth released his solo album, Crazy From the Heat, in 1985. The group had a string of albums—5150 (1986), OU812 (1988), For Unlawful Carnal Knowledge (1991), and Balance (1995)—all reaching #1. Their last release, Van Halen III, hit #3 in 1998.

Steve Winwood

Roll With It peaked at #1 in 1988. Winwood and Jim Capaldi re-formed a version of Traffic in 1994, but when the reception was lukewarm, Winwood began work on another solo album in 1995. In 1997 he released Junction Seven.

ZZ Top®

The "Top" hit the Top 20 with "Gimme All Your Lovin'" in 1984 and "Sleeping Bag" in 1985. They were culled, respectively, from Eliminator and Afterburner, two landmark albums from the early MTV years. The original three members have remained together for more than 30 years. XXX was their last release in 1999.

ADDICTED TO LOVE

Words and Music by
ROBERT PALMER

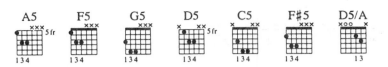

Intro
Moderately ♩ = 112

* Key signature denotes A Mixolydian.

Verse

1. The lights are on but you're not home. Your mind is not your
signs, but you can't read. You're run-nin' at a dif-f'rent

w/ bar *simile on repeats* P.M.

* Play 2nd & 3rd times only.

Addicted to Love - 7 - 1

Pre-Chorus

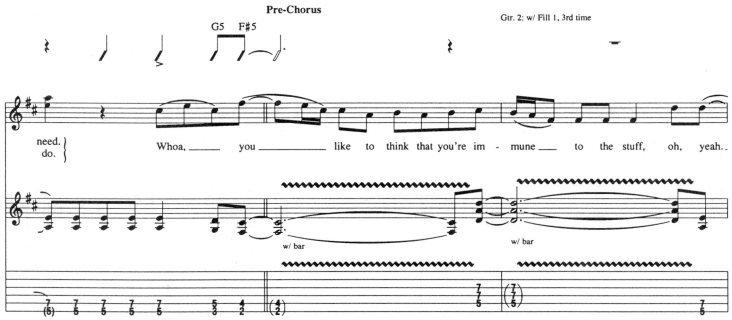

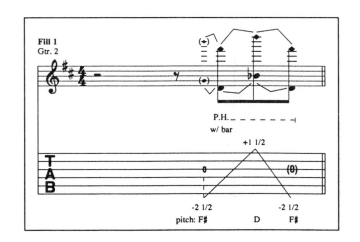

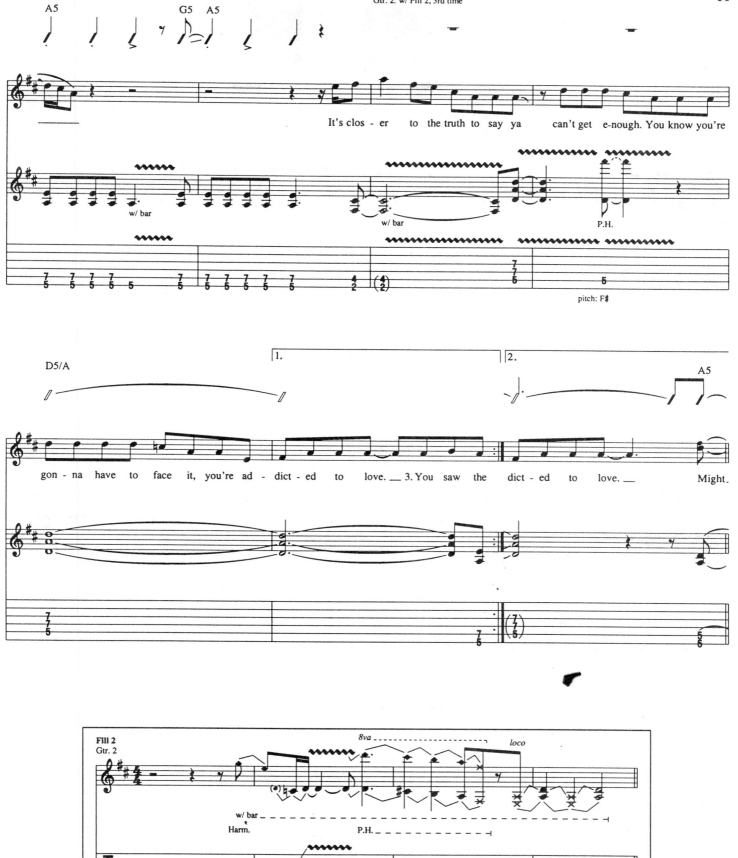

Chorus

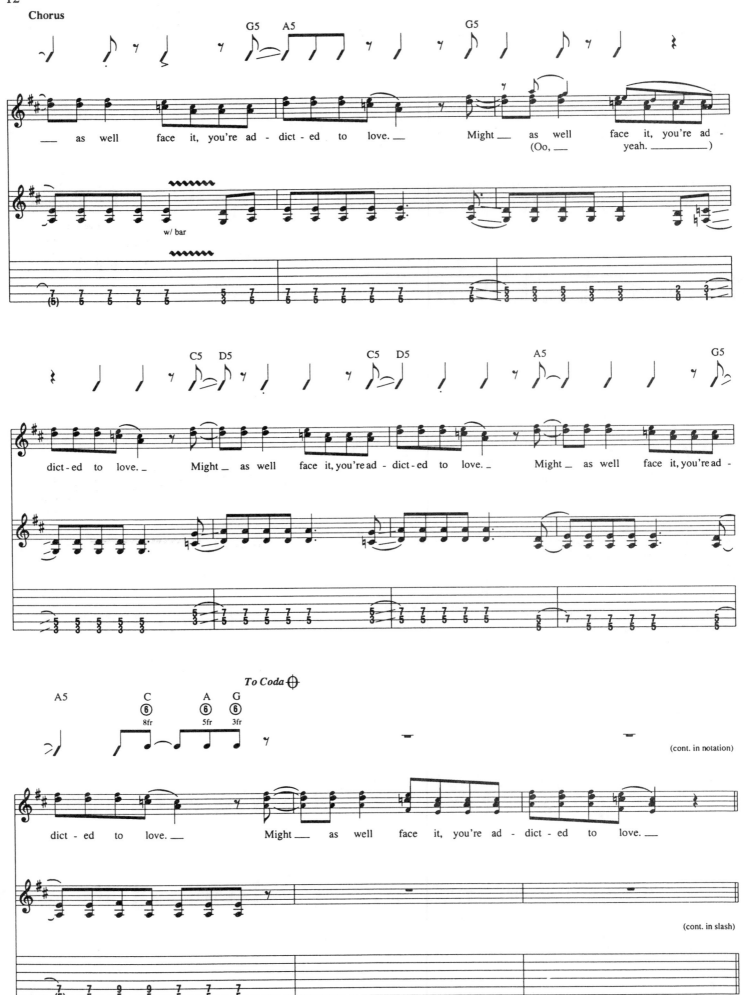

Guitar Solo

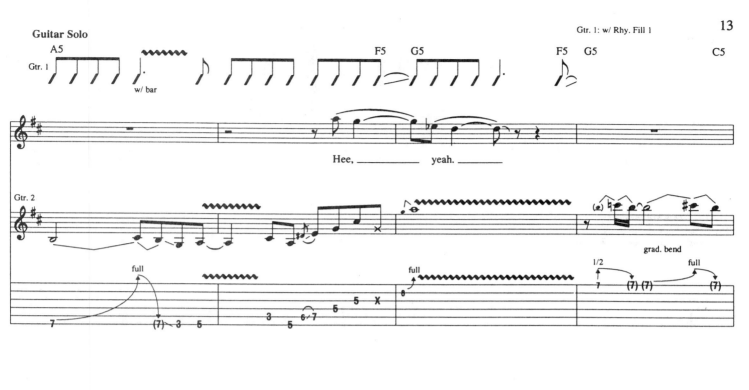

Hee, _____ yeah. _____

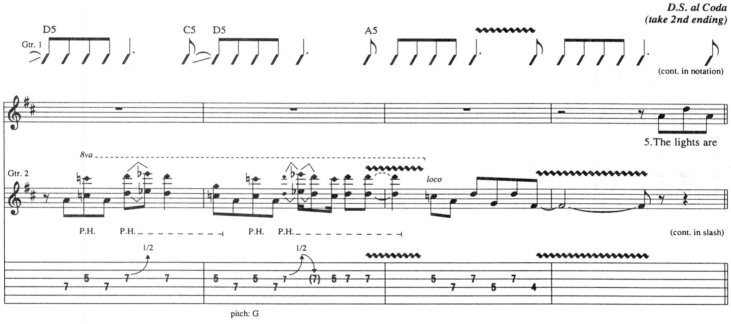

D.S. al Coda
(take 2nd ending)

(cont. in notation)

5. The lights are

(cont. in slash)

pitch: G

Rhy. Fill 1

⊕ *Coda*
Chorus
Begin Fade

Additional Lyrics

5. The lights are on, but you're not home.
   Your will is not your own.
   Your heart sweats, your teeth grind.
   Another kiss and you'll be mine.

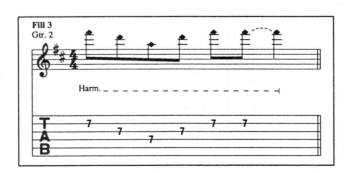

AFRICA

Words and Music by
DAVID PAICH and JEFF PORCARO

Moderately ♩ = 94
Intro:
Gtr. 1 *(12-string acoustic)*

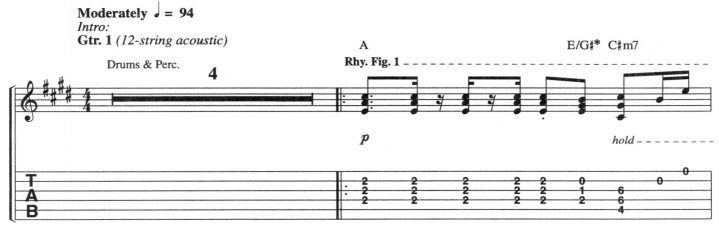

*Bass gtr. plays note to right of slash.

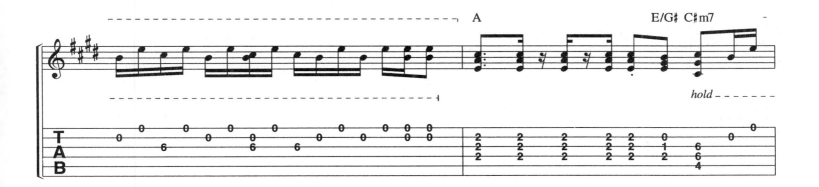

Verse 1:

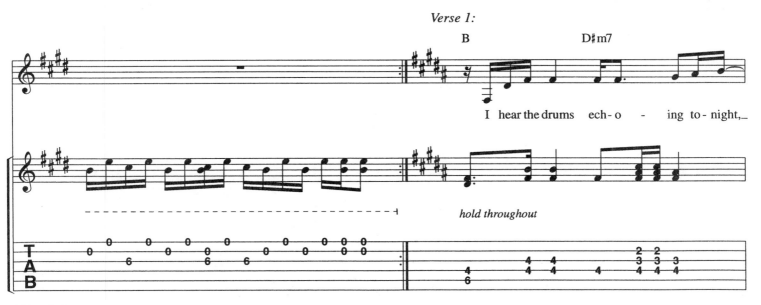

I hear the drums ech-o - ing to-night,__

hold throughout

Africa - 9 - 1

but she hears on - ly whis - pers of some qui - et con - ver - sa -

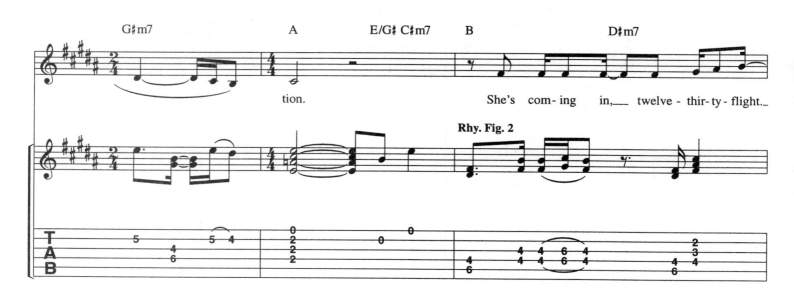

tion. She's com - ing in,__ twelve - thir - ty - flight._

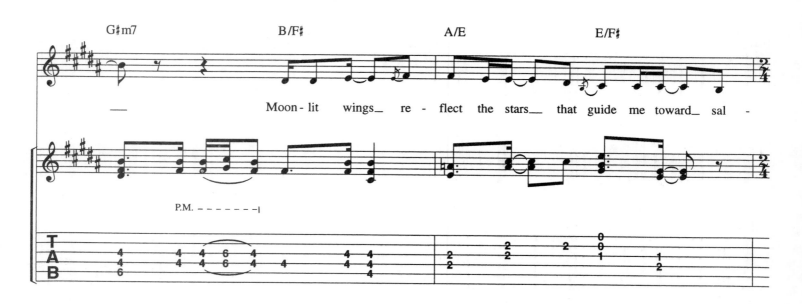

Moon - lit wings_ re - flect the stars_ that guide me toward_ sal -

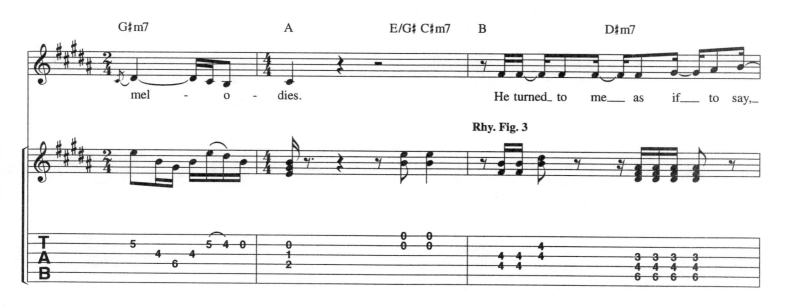

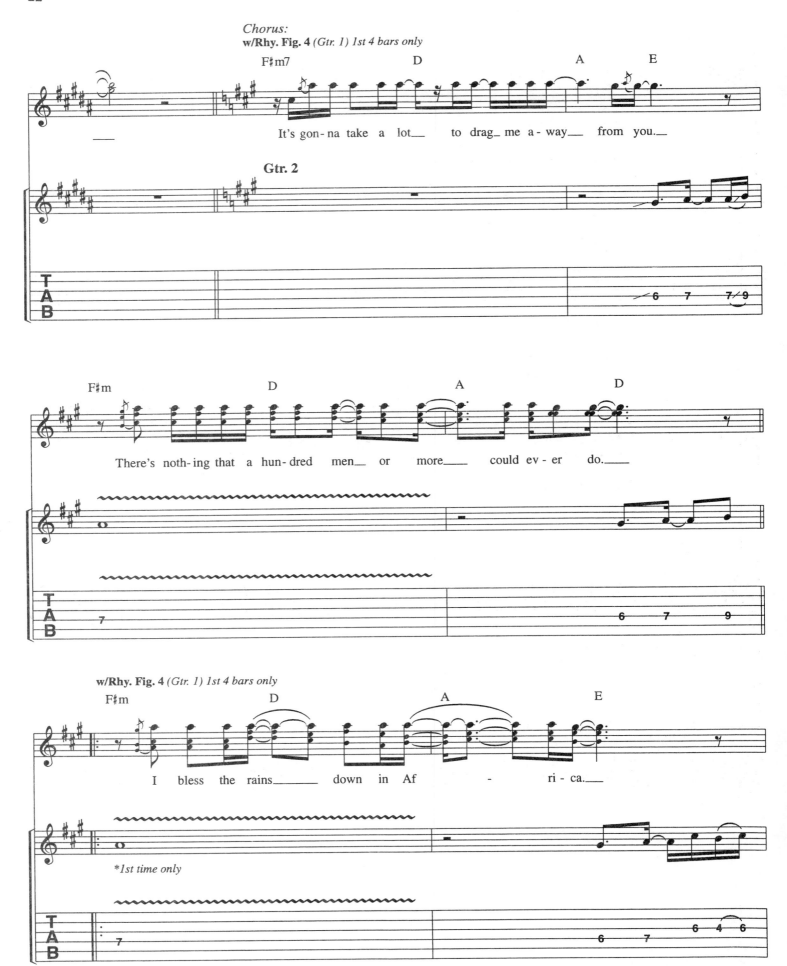

Chorus:
w/Rhy. Fig. 4 *(Gtr. 1) 1st 4 bars only*

It's gon-na take a lot___ to drag___ me a-way___ from you.___

Gtr. 2

There's noth-ing that a hun-dred men___ or more___ could ev - er do.___

w/Rhy. Fig. 4 *(Gtr. 1) 1st 4 bars only*

I bless the rains_____ down in Af - ri - ca.___

1st time only

Lead vocal ad lib. on repeat.

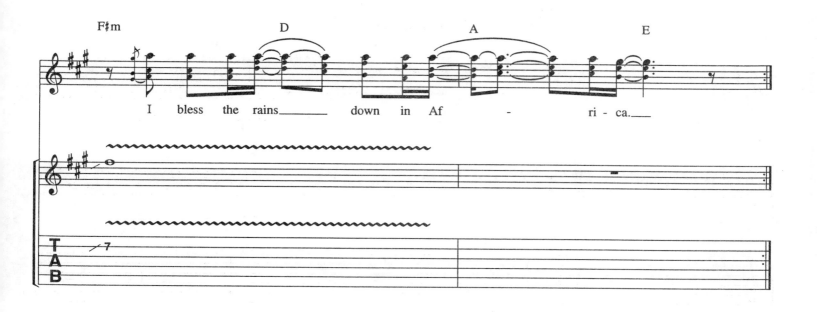

I bless the rains_____ down in Af - ri - ca.____

w/Rhy. Fig. 4 *(Gtr. 1) last 5 bars only*

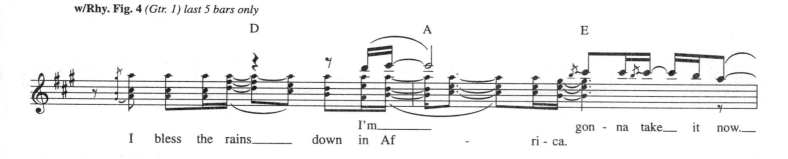

I bless the rains_____ down in Af - ri - ca.

I'm_____ gon - na take__ it now.____

w/Riff A *(Gtr. 2)*

I'm gon - na take some time__ to do__ the things we nev - er have._____

Outro:
w/Rhy. Fig. 1 *(Gtr. 1) 3 times*

Repeat & fade

_____ Ooo._____

BELLA

Words and Music by
CARLOS SANTANA, CHESTER THOMPSON
and STERLING CREW

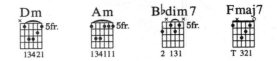

Moderately ♩ = 136

*Kybds. arr. for gtr. throughout.

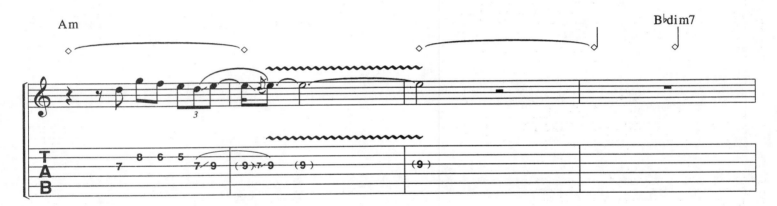

Bella - 6 - 1

Bella - 6 - 4

BLUES FOR SALVADOR

Words and Music by
CARLOS SANTANA and CHESTER THOMPSON

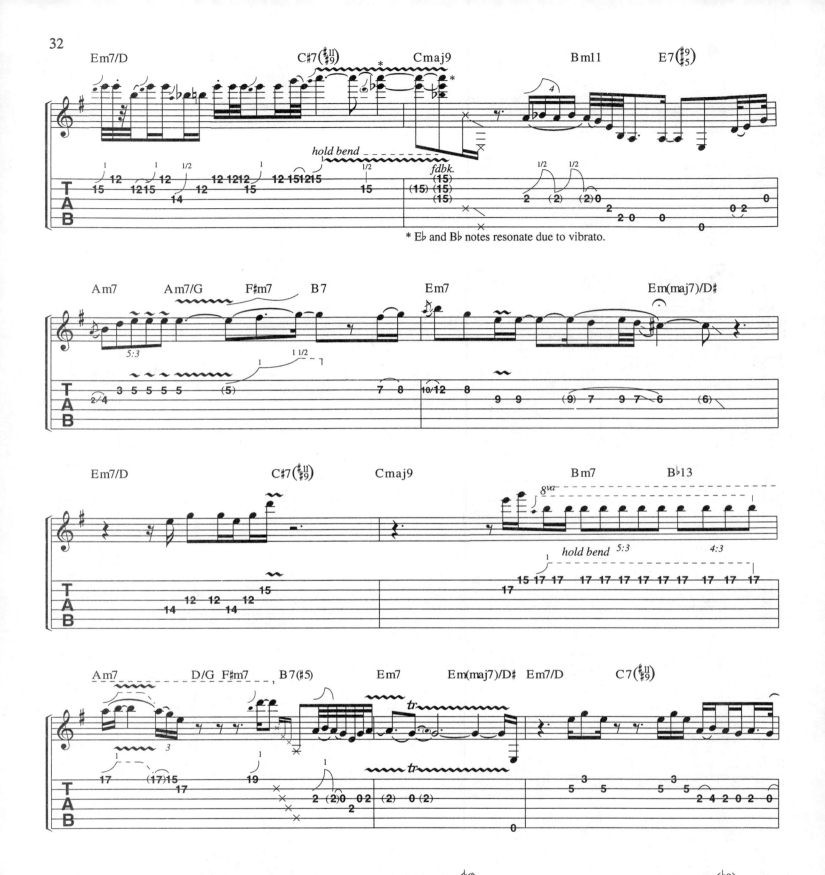

* Eb and Bb notes resonate due to vibrato.

CHEAP SUNGLASSES

Words and Music by
BILLY GIBBONS, DUSTY HILL
and FRANK BEARD

*Bass gtr. pedals G.

38

Cheap Sunglasses – 3 – 2

Verse 2:
Spied a little thing
And I followed her all night.
In a funky fine Levis
And her sweater's kinda tight.
She had a West Coast strut
That was sweet as molasses.
But what really knocked me out
Was her cheap sunglasses.
Oh yeah, oh yeah, oh yeah.
(To Interlude:)

Verse 3:
Now go out and get yourself
Some thick black frames.
With the glass so dark
They won't even know your name.
And the choice is up to you
'Cause they come in two classes:
Rhinestone shades
Or cheap sunglasses.
Oh yeah, oh yeah, oh yeah.
(To Coda)

BURNING DOWN THE HOUSE

Words by
DAVID BYRNE

Music by DAVID BYRNE, CHRIS FRANTZ,
JERRY HARRISON and TINA WEYMOUTH

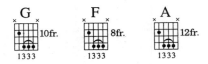

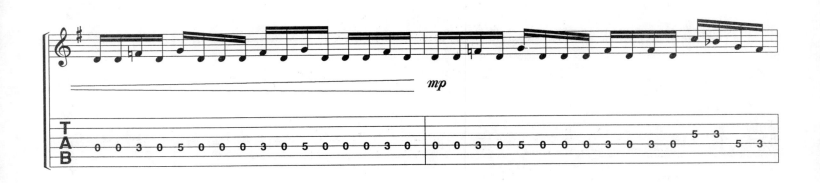

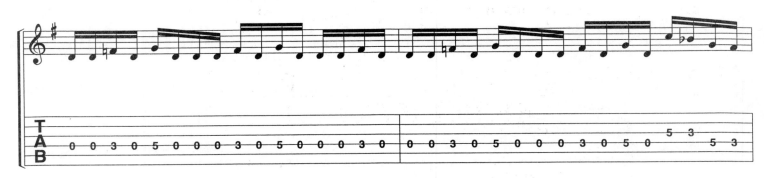

Burning Down the House - 4 - 1

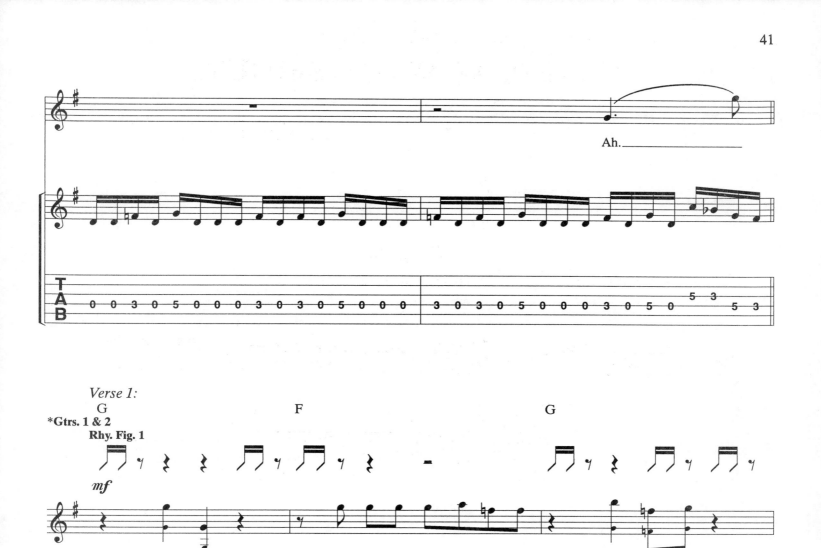

Ah._____

Verse 1:

1. Watch out, you might get what you're af - ter. Cool ba - bies, strange but not a stran - ger. I'm an or - di - nar - y

guy, burn - ing down the house.

2. Hold tight

3. 4. *See additional lyrics*

*Verse 4 only.

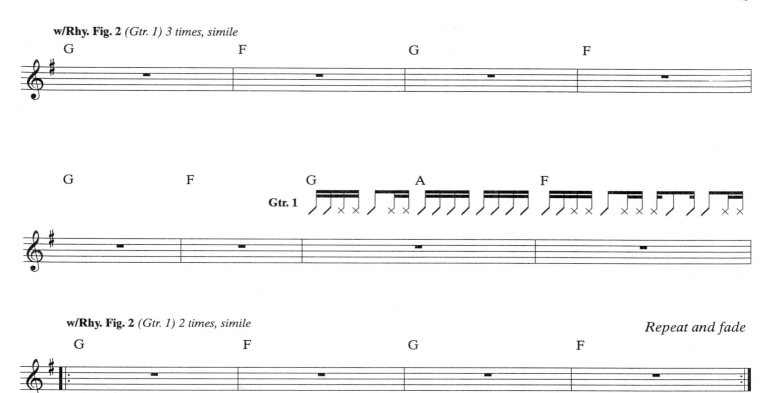

w/Rhy. Fig. 2 *(Gtr. 1) 3 times, simile*

w/Rhy. Fig. 2 *(Gtr. 1) 2 times, simile*

Repeat and fade

Verse 3:
All wet, hey, you might need a rain coat.
Shake down, means walking in broad daylight.
Three hundred sixty-five degrees,
Burning down the house.

Chorus 2:
It was once upon a place, sometimes I listen to myself.
Gonna come in first place.
People on their way to work;
Baby, what do you expect?
Gonna burst into flames.

Verse 4:
My house, down on the haunted alley.
That's right, don't want to hurt nobody.
Some things sure has swept me off my feet,
Burning down the house.

Chorus 3:
No visible means of support
And you have not seen nothing yet.
Everything's stuck together.
And I don't know what you expect,
Staring right into the TV set,
Fightin' fire with fire.
(To Coda)

CALL ME

Words by
DEBORAH HARRY
Music by
GIORGIO MORODER

*1st time only.
**2nd time only.

Verse:

Pre-chorus:

*Two gtrs. arr. for one throughout section.

*Bridge/Synth. Solo:

Elec. Gtr. 1

Ooh,_____ he speaks_ the___ lan - guag - es___ of love.___

Elec. Gtr. 2
Rhy. Fig. 3

end Rhy. Fig. 3

*Vocal 1st time only.

w/Rhy. Fig. 3 (Elec. Gtr. 2) simile

Ooh,_____ a - mo - re,___ chia - ma - mi,_

chia - ma - mi.   Ooh,_____ a - pelle_ moi,_

48

*This riff 1st time only.

DANCING WITH MYSELF

Words and Music by
BILLY IDOL and TONY JAMES

*Ld. vcl. from 2nd time on (ad lib. simile on repeats);
"Dancing with myself" bkgd. vcl. from 2nd time on.

DEVIL INSIDE

Words and Music by
ANDREW FARRISS and
MICHAEL HUTCHENCE

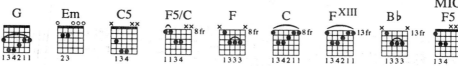

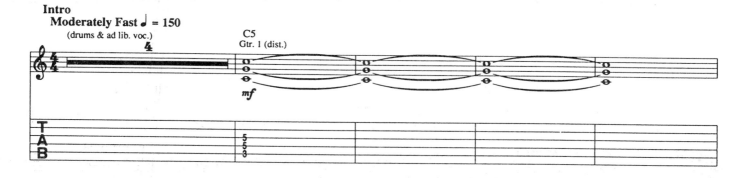

1. Here come the wo- man, ___ with the look in her eye. ___

Devil Inside - 9 - 1

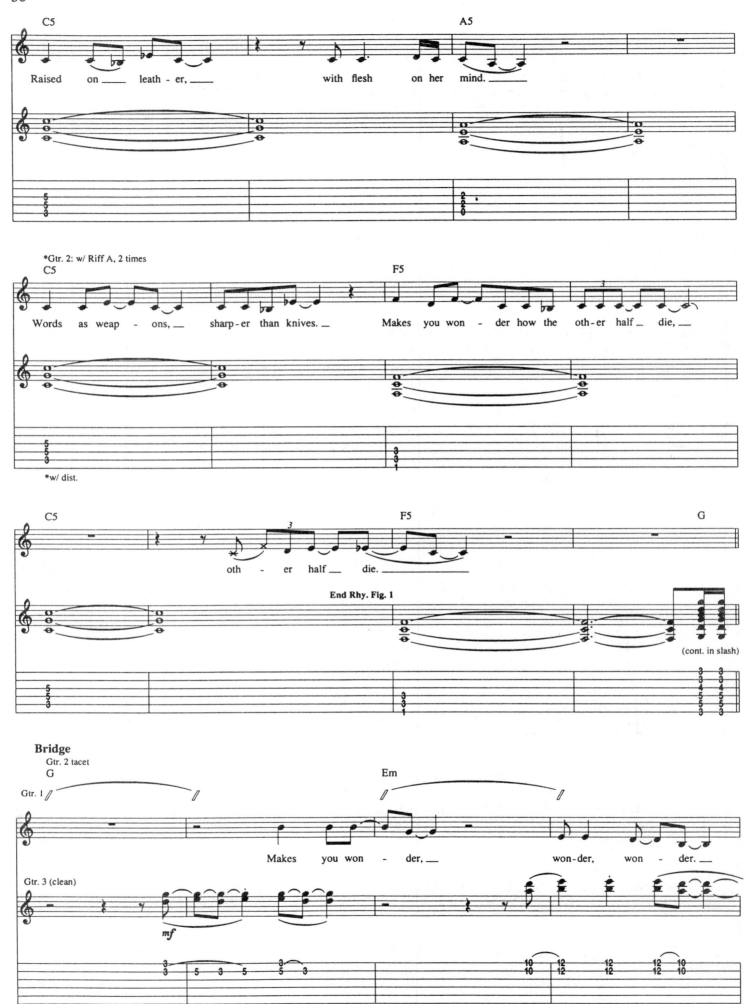

58

Interlude

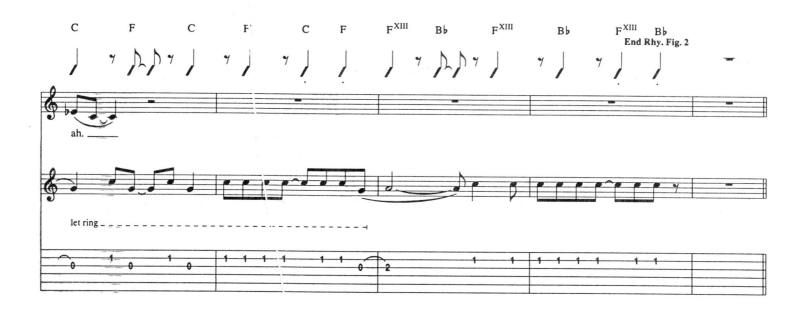

Guitar Solo

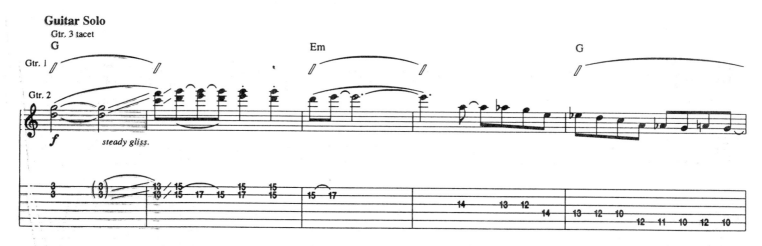

Words are weap - ons,__ sharp - er than knives.__ Makes you won - der how the

Chorus

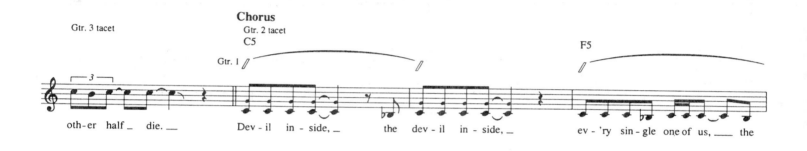

oth-er half _ die. __ Dev - il in - side, __ the dev - il in - side, _ ev - 'ry sin - gle one of us, ___ the

dev - il in - side. _ Dev - il in - side, _ dev-il in - side, _ ev - 'ry sin - gle one of us, ___ the

dev - il in - side. _ The dev - il in - side, _ dev - il in - side, _ ev - 'ry sin - gle one of us, ___ the

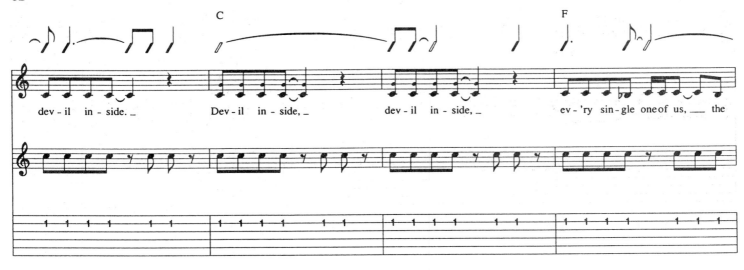

Outro
Gtr. 1: w/ Rhy. Fig. 2, till fade

The dev - il in - side. _____ Yeah, yeah, yeah. _____

Oh. _____ The dev - il in - side. _____

Gtr. 2: w/ Fill 1, 8 times
w/ voc. ad lib., till fade

Play 8 Times and Fade

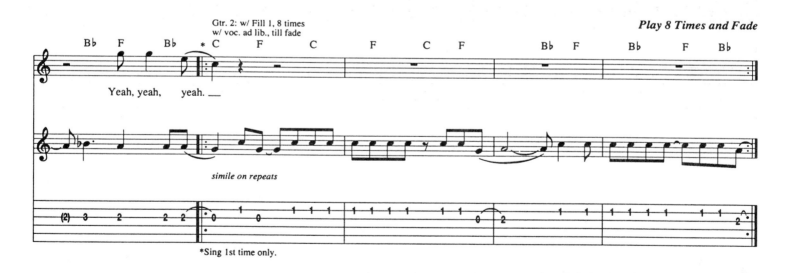

Yeah, yeah, yeah. ___

simile on repeats

*Sing 1st time only.

Fill 1
Gtr. 2

DRIVE

Words and Music by
RIC OCASEK

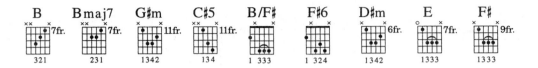

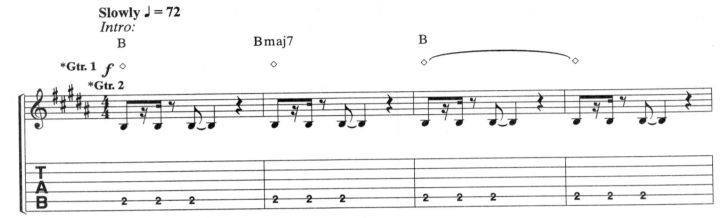

*All gtrs. are keybds. arr. for gtr. throughout.

**Rhy. Fig. 1 includes both gtrs.

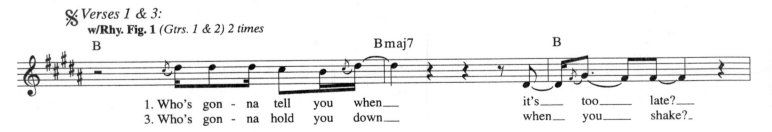

1. Who's gon - na tell you when___ it's___ too___ late?___
3. Who's gon - na hold you down___ when___ you___ shake?_

Who's gon - na tell___ you things___ aren't___
Who's gon - na come___ a - round___ when___

Drive - 6 - 4

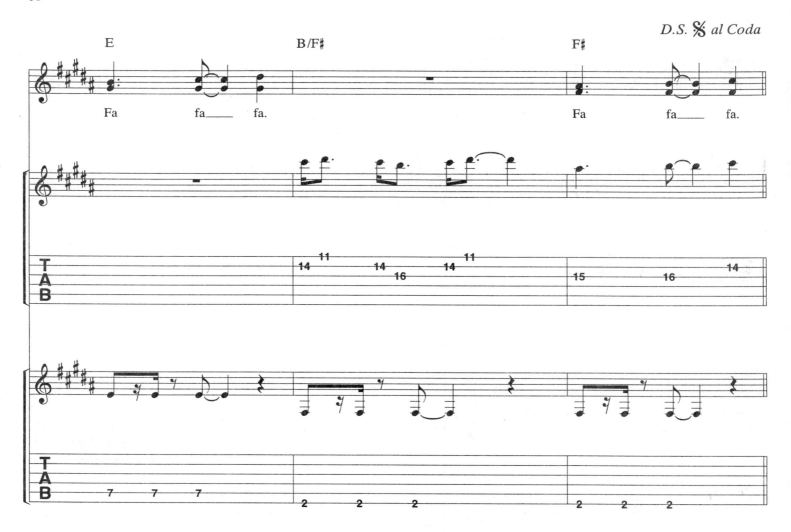

Ho,_____ you know you can't go on_____ think-in'

noth - in's wrong._____ Who's gon - na drive_ you home_

_____ to - night?__

Drive - 6 - 6

ERUPTION

Words and Music by
EDWARD VAN HALEN, ALEX VAN HALEN,
MICHAEL ANTHONY and DAVID LEE ROTH

Tune down 1/2 step:
⑥ = Eb ③ = Gb
⑤ = Ab ② = Bb
④ = Db ① = Eb

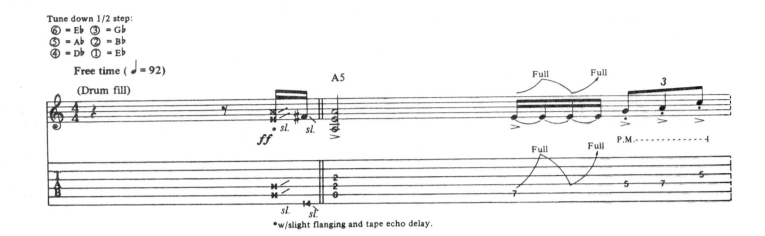

*w/slight flanging and tape echo delay.

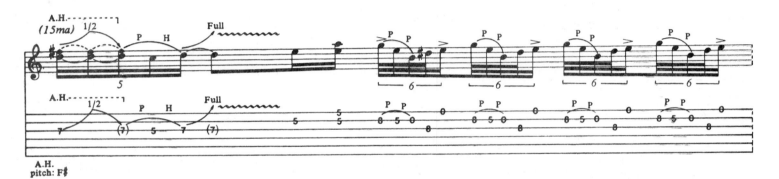

A.H.
pitch: F#

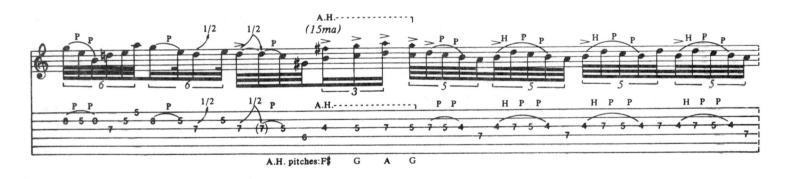

A.H. pitches: F# G A G

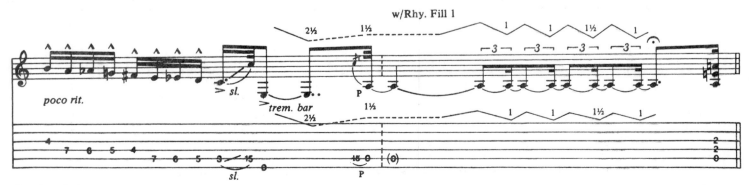

Eruption - 4 - 1

*Release finger pressure when arriving at 19fr. at end of slide to sound F♯ natural harmonic.

Rhy. Fill 1

Overdubbed gtr.

*Slightly rushed.

*Tap open low E at 12fr.
to produce octave harmonic.

Fdbk. pitch: B

**Univox tape echo runaway feedback effect.

Eruption - 4 - 4

EVERY ROSE HAS ITS THORN

Words and Music by
B. MICHAELS, B. DALL,
C.C. DEVILLE and R. ROCKETT

Every Rose Has Its Thorn - 9 - 1

Every Rose Has Its Thorn - 9 - 2

ev - ery cow - boy___ sings his sad, sad___ song,

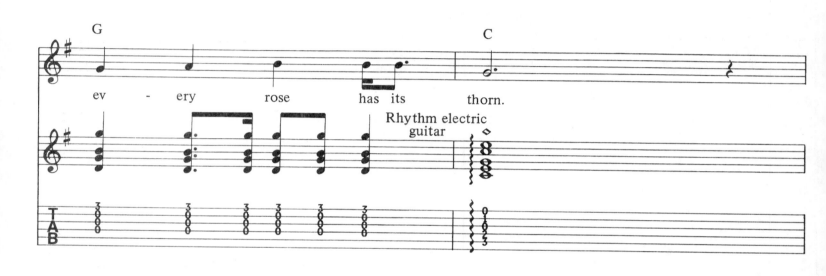

ev - ery rose has its thorn.

Rhythm electric guitar

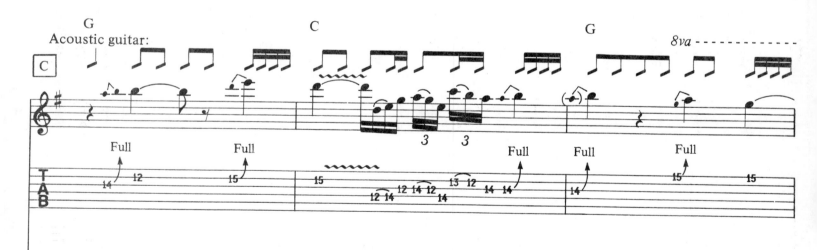

Acoustic guitar:

C

8va - - - - - - - - - - - -

Full Full Full Full Full

Electric guitar (clean sound)

78

Every Rose Has Its Thorn - 9 - 8

EYES WITHOUT A FACE

Words and Music by
BILLY IDOL and STEVE STEVENS

Eyes Without a Face - 5 - 1

Eyes Without a Face - 5 - 3

Verse 3:
Resume verse fig. simile

Eyes Without a Face - 5 - 5

FOOLIN'

Words and Music by
STEVE CLARK, JOE ELLIOTT
and R.J. LANGE

*Alternate Tuning:

⑥ = D   ③ = G
⑤ = A   ② = B
④ = D   ① = E

Moderately ♩ = 113

Intro:

Strings **Gtr. 3** **Rhy. Fig. 1** Am(9)   F(♯4)/A   Fmaj7(♯4)/A   Am(9)   F(♯4)/A
(Acoustic)

hold throughout

*Alternate tuning for Gtr. 1 only.

Verse:
w/Rhy. Fig. 1 *(Gtr. 3) 2 times*

Fmaj7(♯4)/A   Am(9)   Fmaj7(♯4)/A

end Rhy. Fig. 1

1. La - dy Luck ____ nev - er smiles, ____ so

Am(9)   F(♯4)/A   Fmaj7(♯4)/A   Am(9)   F(♯4)/A   Fmaj7(♯4)/A

lend your love ____ to me a - while. ____ Do with me ____ what you will, ____

w/Rhy. Fig. 1 *(Gtr. 3) 2 times*

Am(9)   F(♯4)/A   Fmaj7(♯4)/A   Am(9)   F(♯4)/A   Fmaj7(♯4)/A

break the spell, ____ take your fill. ____ On and on ____ we ____ rode the storm, ____
2. *See additional lyrics*

Am(9)   F(♯4)/A   Fmaj7(♯4)/A   Am(9)   F(♯4)/A

the flame _ has died   and the fire has gone. ____ Oh, ____ this emp - ty bed is a night ____

Foolin' – 8 – 1

Bridge:

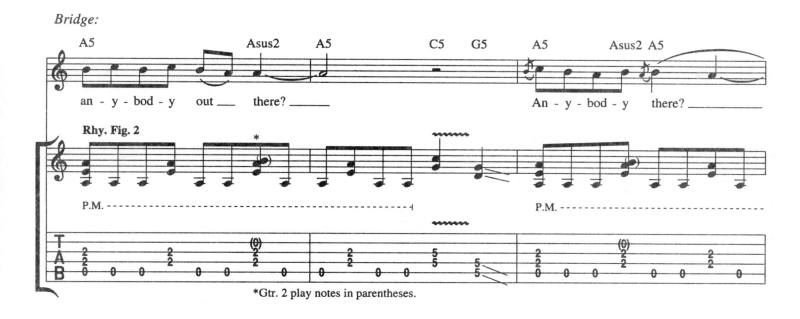

*Gtr. 2 play notes in parentheses.

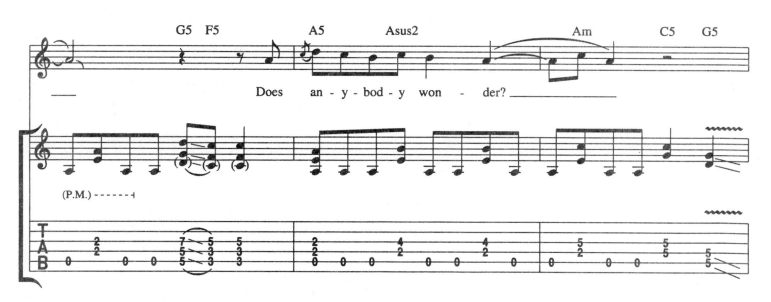

*Depress bar before striking note and gradually pull up.

Coda

Ah! __ No! __ I'm not fool-in' my-self. _____ Fool-in' my-self, __

Verse 2:
Close your eyes,
Don't run and hide,
Easy love is no easy ride.
Just wakin' up to what we had
Could stop good love from goin' bad.
(To Bridge:)

GOOD TIMES ROLL

Words and Music by
RIC OCASEK

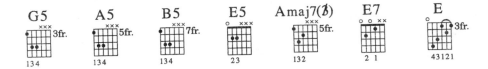

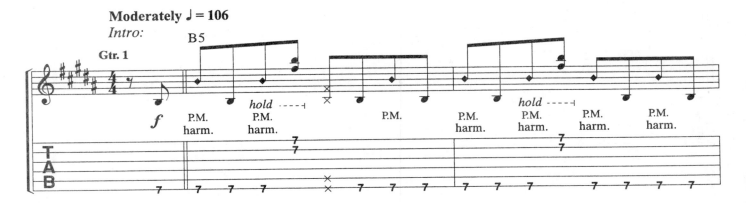

Good Times Roll - 12 - 1

A5   B5

good times___ roll.   Let them make you   a   clown.

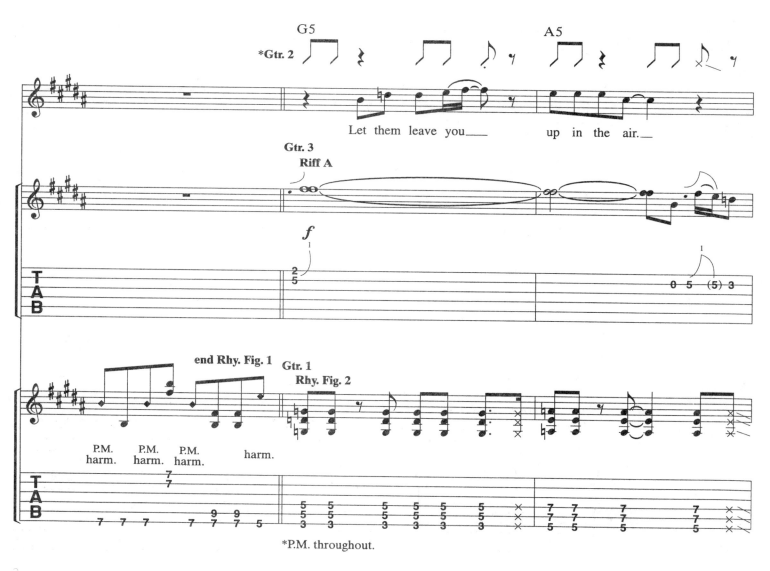

G5   A5

*Gtr. 2

Let them leave you___   up in the air.___

Gtr. 3
Riff A

end Rhy. Fig. 1   Gtr. 1
Rhy. Fig. 2

*P.M. throughout.

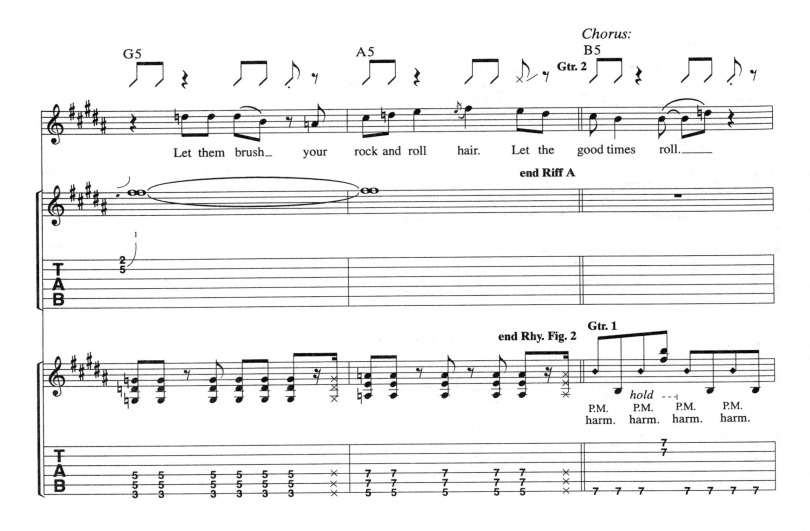

*Synth. arr. for gtr. throughout.

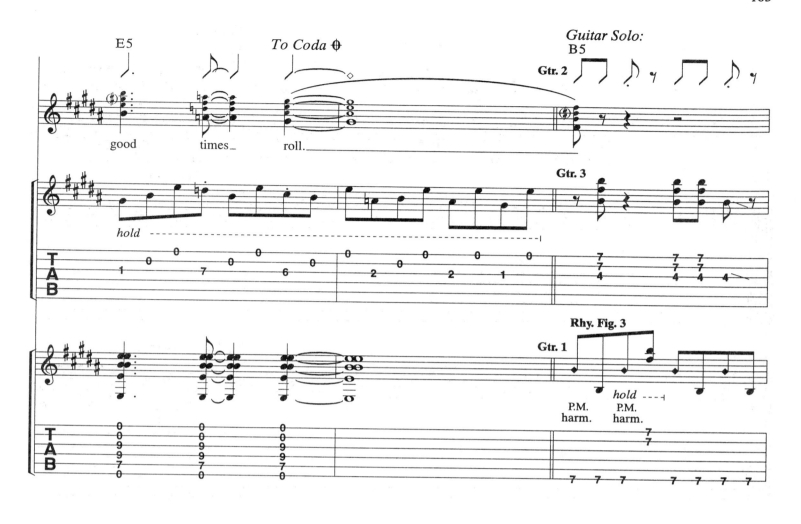

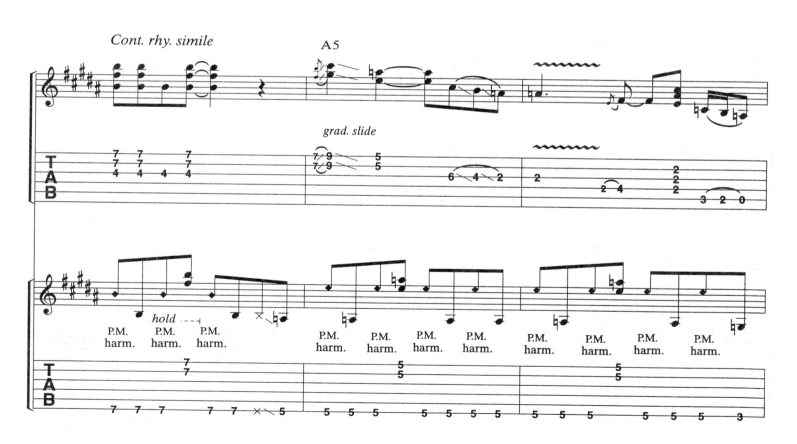

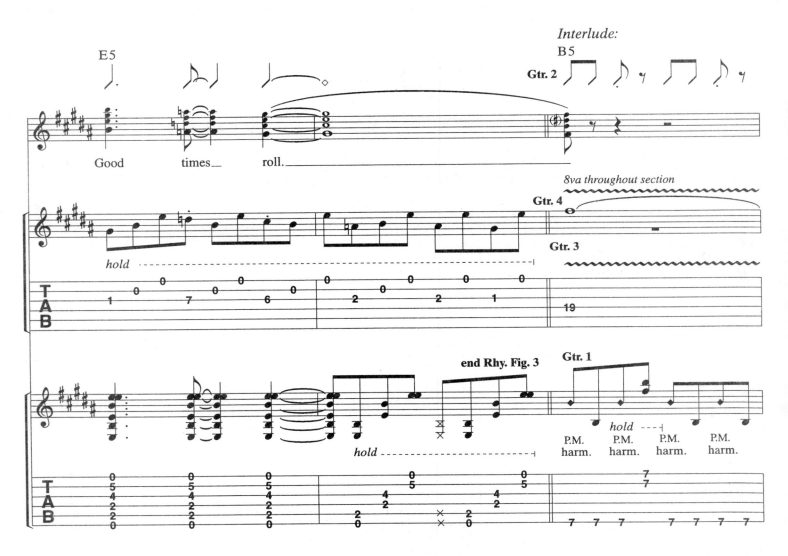

D.S. %. al Coda

Out Chorus:

w/Rhy. Fig. 3 (Gtr. 1) simile

*Vocals ad lib. on repeats.
†Ad lib. simile on repeats.

Verse 3:
If the illusion is real,
Let them give you a ride.
If they got thunder appeal,
Let them be on your side.
(To Pre-Chorus:)

HEART OF GLASS

Words and Music by
DEBORAH HARRY and CHRIS STEIN

just   no good,   you teas - ing like__ you do.__

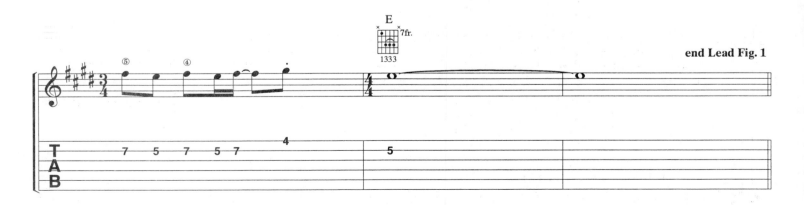

HERE COMES MY GIRL

Words and Music by
TOM PETTY and MIKE CAMPBELL

Here Comes My Girl – 3 – 2

114

Verse 2:
Every now and then I get down to the end of the day,
I have to stop and ask myself why I've done it.
It just seems so useless to have to work so hard
And nothing ever really seems to come from it.
And then she looks me in the eye and says,
"We're gonna last forever."
Man, you know I can't begin to doubt it.
You know it just feels so good and so free and so right.
I know we ain't never gonna change our minds about it.
(To Chorus:)

Verse 3:
Every time it seems like there ain't nothin' left no more,
I find myself havin' to reach out and grab hold of something.
Then I just catch myself wondering, waiting and
Worrying about some silly little thing that don't add up to nothing.
And then she looks me in the eye and says,
"We're gonna last forever."
Man, you know I can't begin to doubt it.
You know it just feels so good and so free and so right.
I know we ain't never gonna change our minds about it.
(To Chorus:)

HOLD THE LINE

Words and Music by
DAVID PAICH

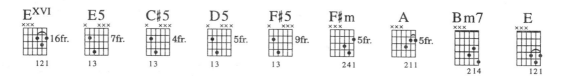

*Piano arr. for gtr.

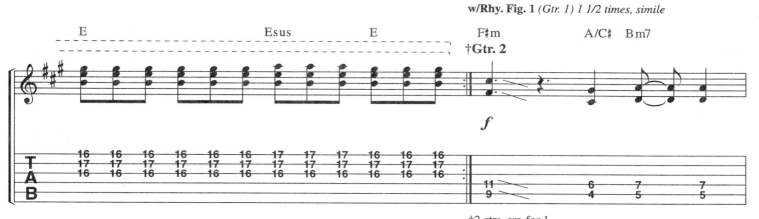

†2 gtrs. arr. for 1.

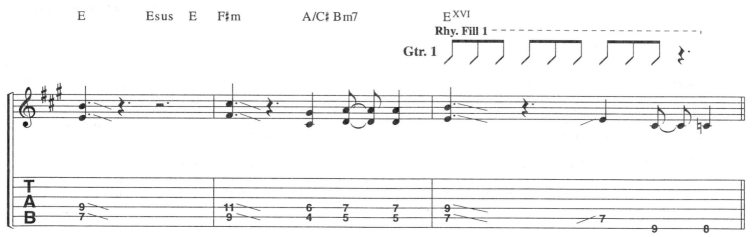

Hold the Line - 9 - 1

Verse:
w/Fill 1 *(Gtr. 3)* & *(Gtrs. 3, 4 & 5) Verse 3 only (end of Solo)*

1. *It's* not in the way that *you* hold me,
2. 3. *See additional lyrics*

*Chords derived from piano.
†Vibrato on Verse 2 only.

it's not in the way you say you care.

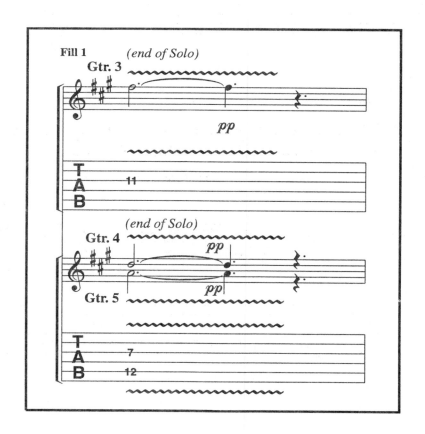

118

*Cont. in slashes

*Verse 2 only.

Hold the Line - 9 - 4

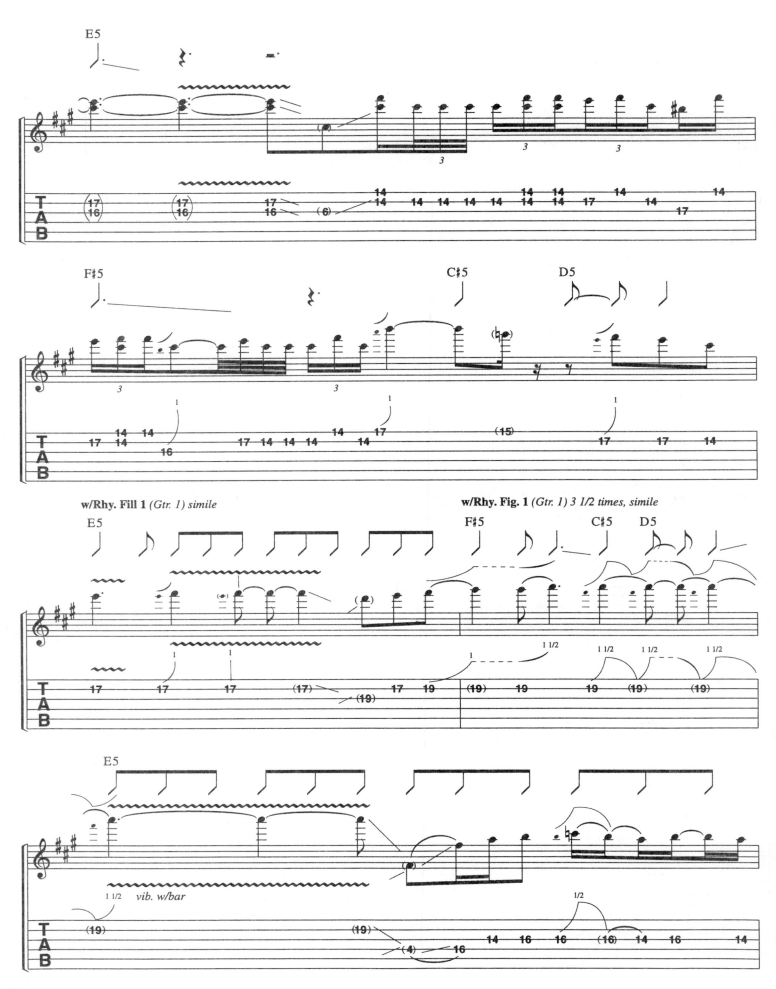

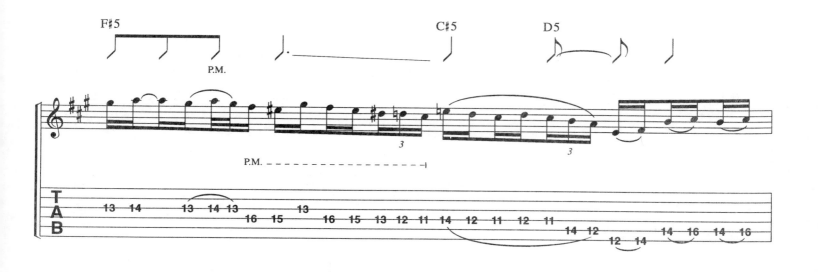

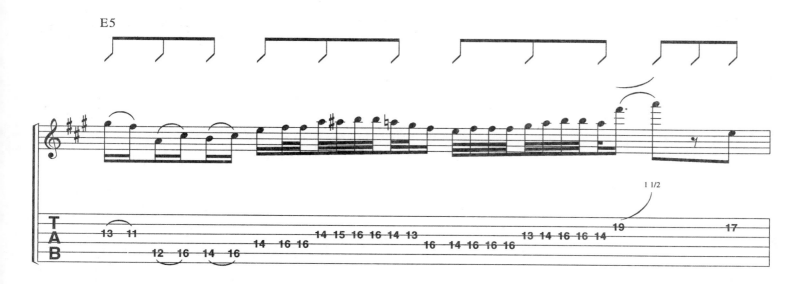

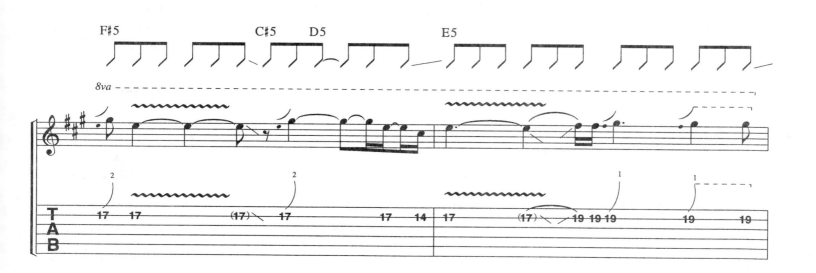

Verses 2 & 3:
It's not in the words that you told me,
It's not in the way you say you're mine, ooh.
It's not in the way that you came back to me,
It's not in the way that your love set me free.
It's not in the way you look, or the
Things that you say that you'll do.
(To Chorus:)

HIGHER LOVE

Words and Music by
STEVE WINWOOD and WILL JENNINGS

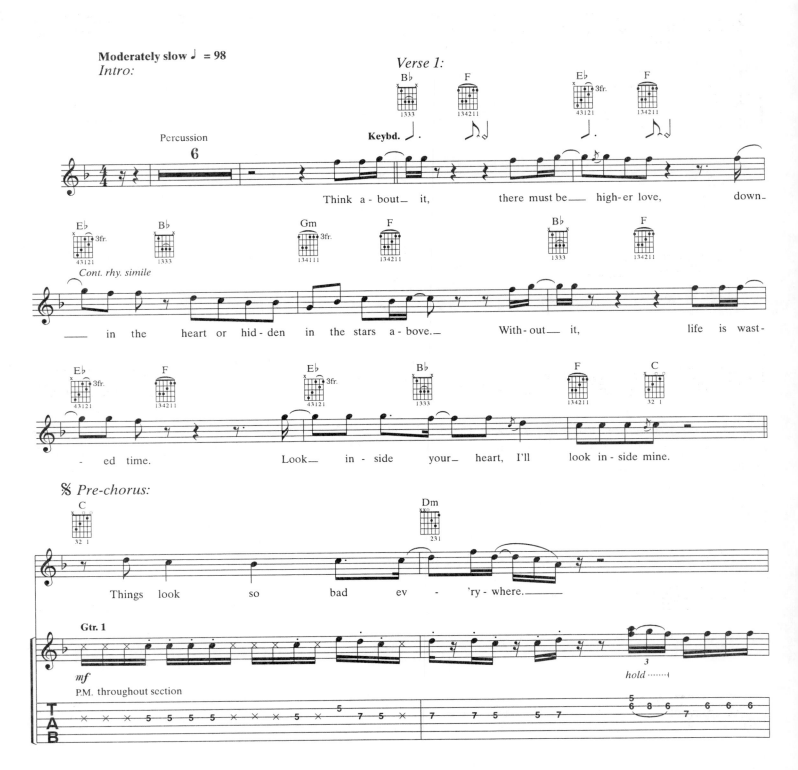

Higher Love - 8 - 1

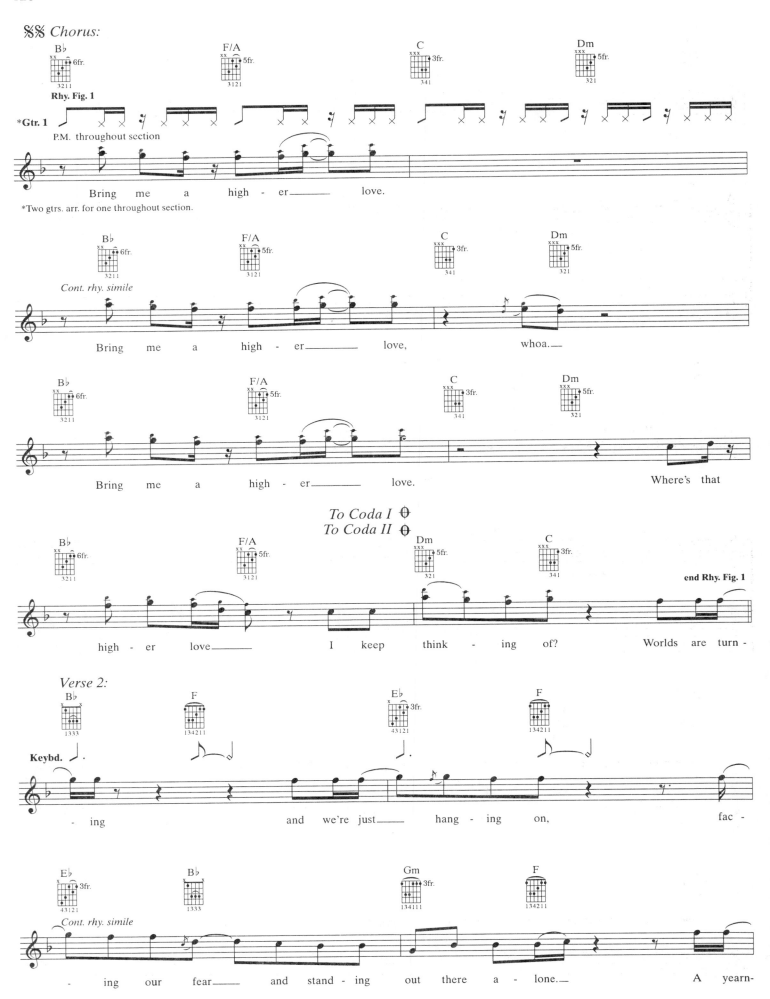

Higher Love - 8 - 4

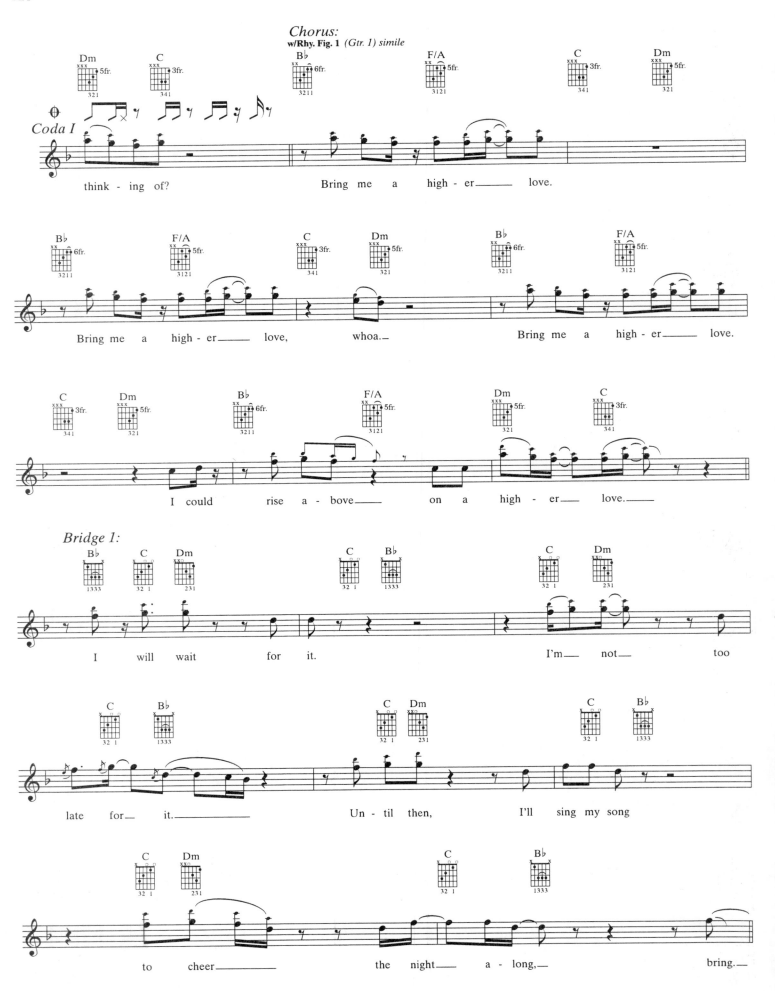

Let me feel___ that love___ come o - ver me.

Cont. rhy. simile

Let me feel_____ how strong it could be.

Interlude:
N.C.
Keybd.

D.S. 𝄋𝄋 *al Coda II*

Oh._____

Interlude:

*Gtr. 1
P.M. throughout section

Coda II

think - ing of?

*Two gtrs. arr. for one throughout section.

I WANNA BE SEDATED

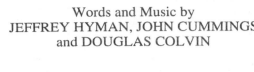

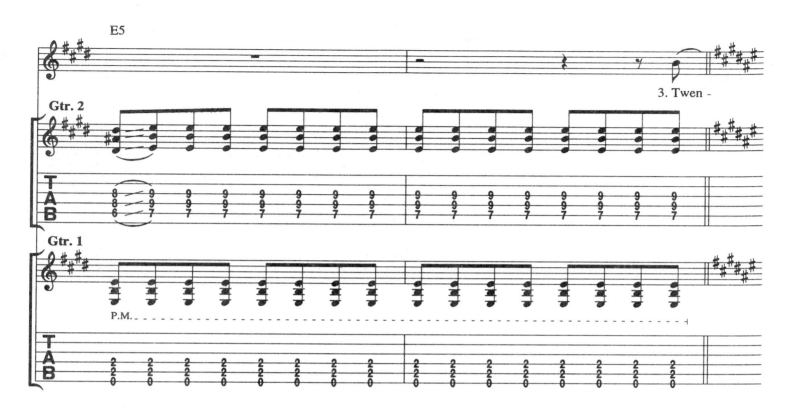

𝄋 *Verses 3 & 4:*

I WANT ACTION

Words and Music by
B.DALL, C.C.DEVILLE,
B.MICHAELS and R.ROCKETT

I Want Action – 7 – 2

MISS YOU IN A HEARTBEAT

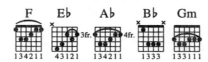

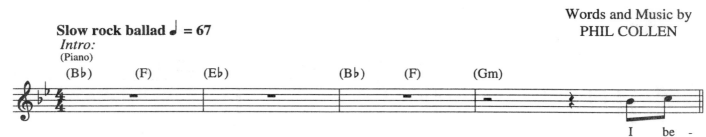

Words and Music by
PHIL COLLEN

Slow rock ballad ♩ = 67

Intro:
(Piano)

I be -

Verse 1:

lieve   that there's some-thing deep in - side ___   that should - n't be from time to

time. ___   I sure found out, ___   for love was such a crime. _____

Pre-Chorus 1:
Rhy. Fig. 1

The more you care,   the more you fall. ___   No need to wor - ry,   no

Gtr. 1 *w/o distortion*

Rhy. Fig. 1A

*Acoustic gtr.

Miss You in a Heartbeat - 7 - 1

146

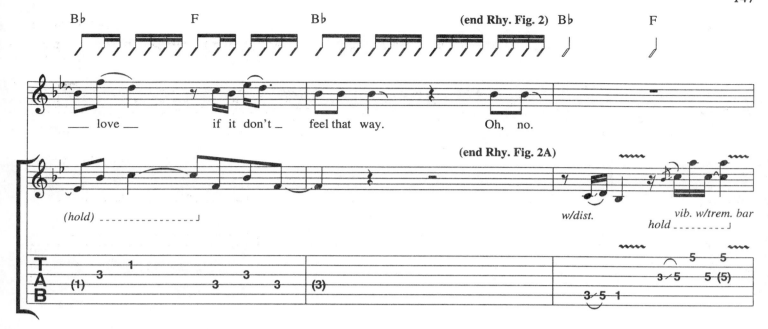

Verse 2:

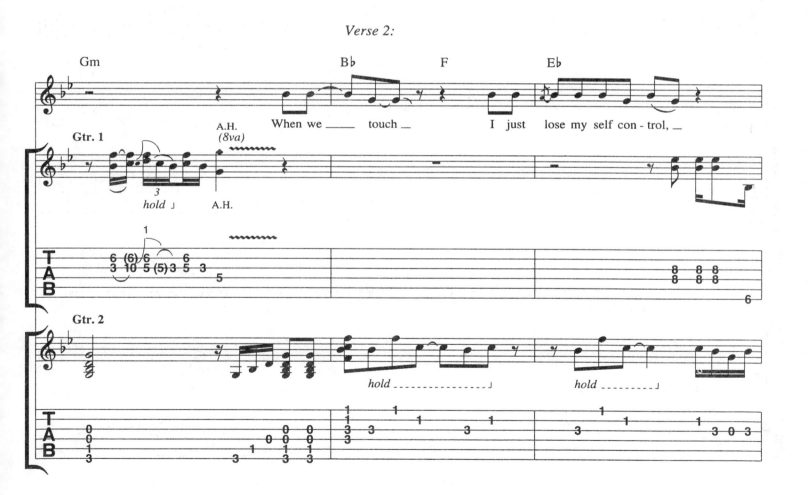

Pre-Chorus 2:
w/Rhy. Fig. 1 & 1A

No need to wor-ry, no need to turn _ a - way 'cause it don't mat - ter _____ any - y -

Chorus 2:
w/Rhy. Fig. 2 & 2A

way, ba - by. Oooh, _____ I miss you in a heart - beat.

Oooh. _____ Yeah, ___ I miss you right a - way. _ Oooh, _____ I

miss you in a heart - beat. 'Cause it ain't _ love _ if it don't _ feel that way. Now,

Bridge:
Gtr. 1

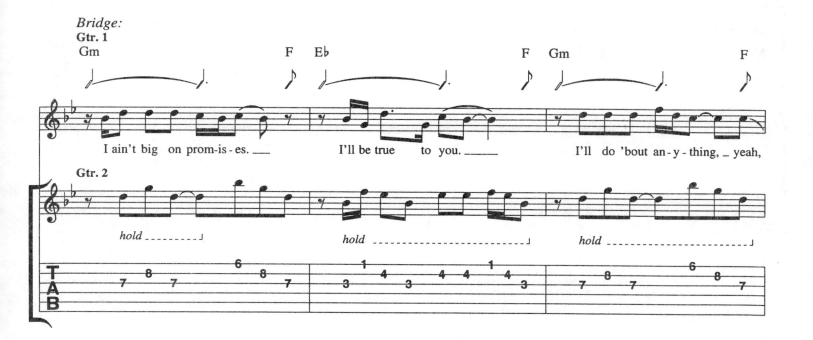

I ain't big on prom - is - es. ___ I'll be true to you. ___ I'll do 'bout an - y - thing, _ yeah,

Gtr. 2

hold _____
hold _____
hold _____

Chorus 3:
w/Rhy. Fig. 2 & 2A (first 7 bars)

(Oooh,_____)   I   miss you   in   a   heart - beat.   (Oooh. _____)

Yeah, ____   I'd

miss you right a - way.____   (Oooh,__)   (I   miss you   in   a   heart -   beat.)

Oh, __   miss you   in   a   heart - beat. 'Cause it ain't_

rit.

___ love _____   if   it   don't __   feel   that   way.

Gtr. 2

Bb

Gtr. 1

rit.

JUMP

Words and Music by
EDWARD VAN HALEN, ALEX VAN HALEN,
MICHAEL ANTHONY and DAVID LEE ROTH

Jump - 6 - 1

*Chord names derived from bass and synth. (next 8 bars).
**Tune down 1/2 step. Music sounds as written.

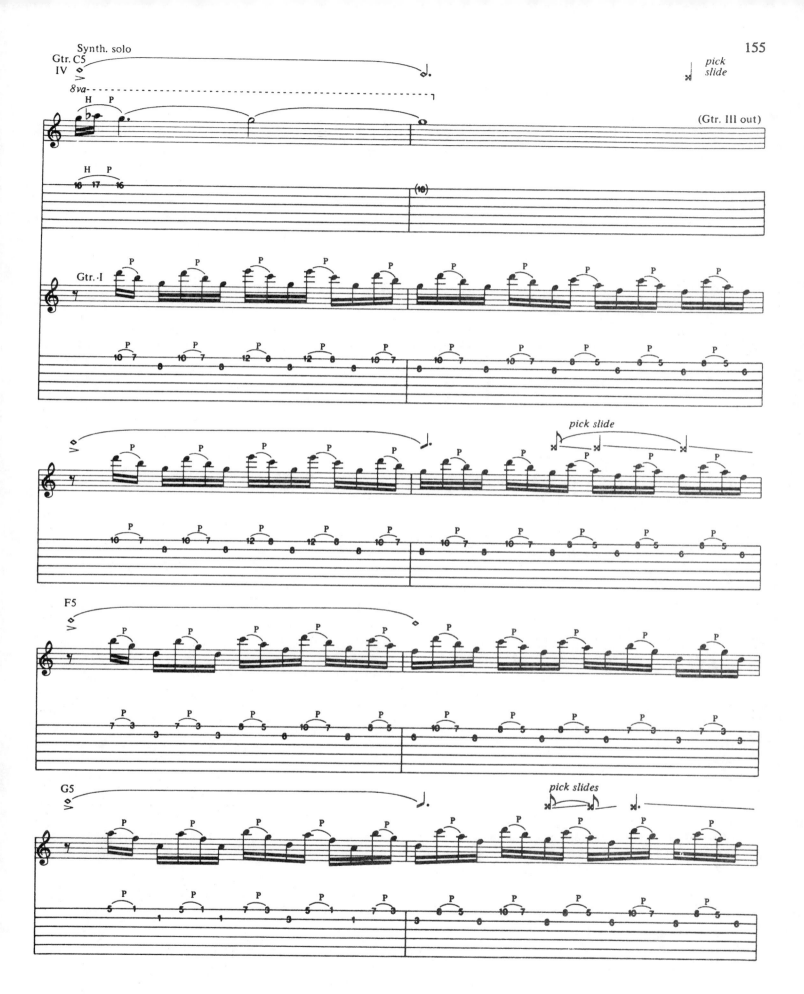

*T =Tap w/R.H. index finger.
Ⓣ=Tap w/R.H. ring finger.
Ⓟ=Pull-off to R.H. index finger.

(Gtr. IV out)

w/Riff A

Out-chorus
w/Riff A (3 times)

Might as well

jump. (Jump!)   Go a-head and   jump._   Get in and

Gtr. II

P.M.

JUST WHAT I NEEDED

Words and Music by
RIC OCASEK

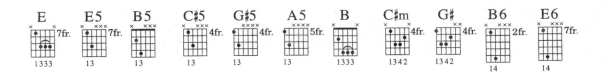

Moderately ♩ = 124

Intro:

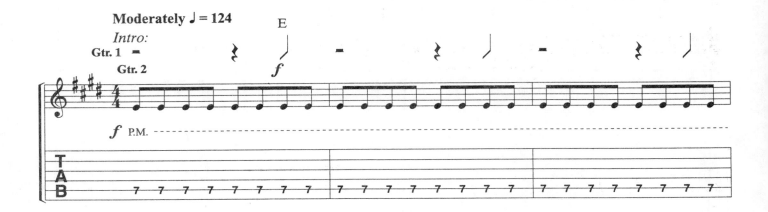

Verse 1:

I don't mind you

Just What I Needed - 10 - 1

Just What I Needed - 10 - 2

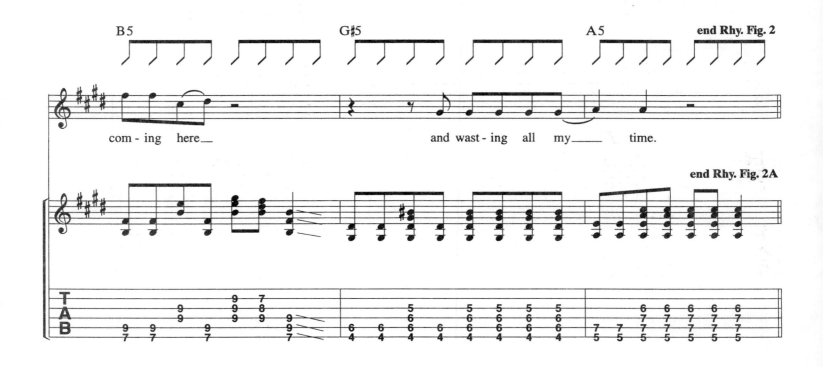

com - ing here___   and wast - ing all my___ time.

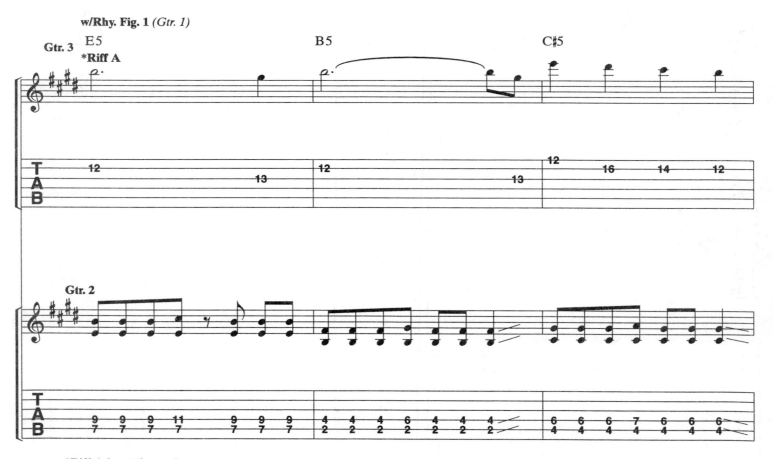

*Riff A is synth. arr. for gtr.

MORE THAN WORDS

Lyrics and Music by
BETTENCOURT, CHERONE

Tune down:
⑥ = E♭ ③ = G♭
⑤ = A♭ ② = B♭
④ = D♭ ① = E♭

Intro:
Ac. Moderate ♩ = 93
Gtr.

*Tap the top of the guitar on 2 and 4 of each measure
with all four fingers of the right hand.

Rhy. Fig. 1

Verse 1:
w/Rhy. Fig. 1

1. Say-in' "I__ love_____ you" is not the words__ I want__ to__ hear__ from you.__
2. *See additional lyrics.*

w/Rhy. Fig. 1 (*1st 3 bars*)

__ It's not that I__ want_____ you not to say.__ But if you__ on - ly knew

More Than Words - 6 - 1

172

More Than Words - 6 - 5

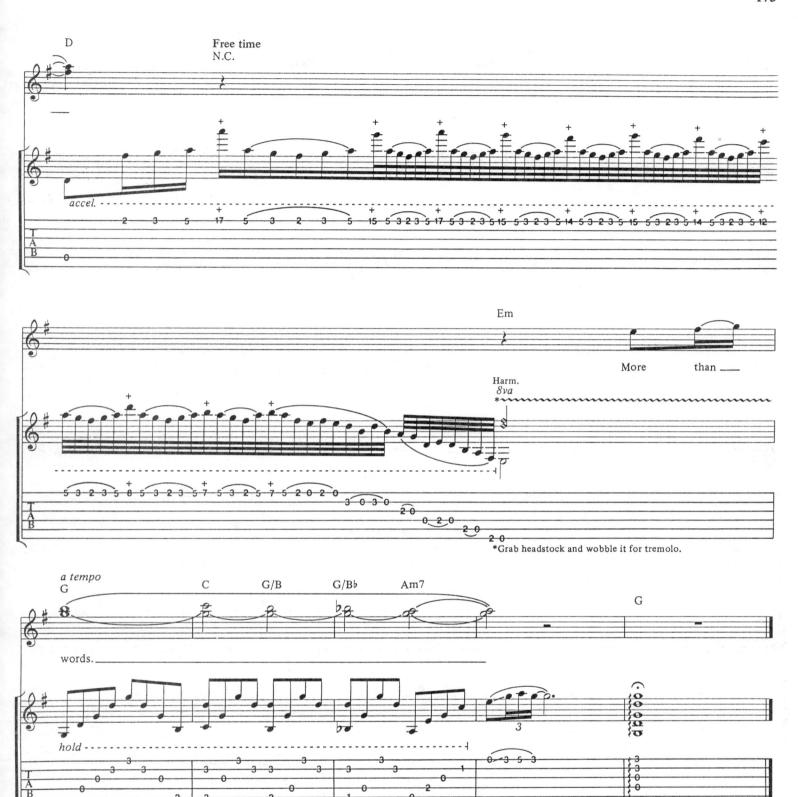

*Grab headstock and wobble it for tremolo.

Verse 2:
Now that I have tried to talk to you
And make you understand.
All you have to do is close your eyes
And just reach out your hands.
And touch me, hold me close, don't ever let me go.
More than words is all I ever needed to show.
Then you wouldn't have to say
That you love me 'cause I'd already know.

MY BEST FRIEND'S GIRL

Words and Music by
RIC OCASEK

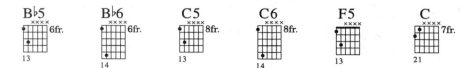

Moderately ♩ = 116

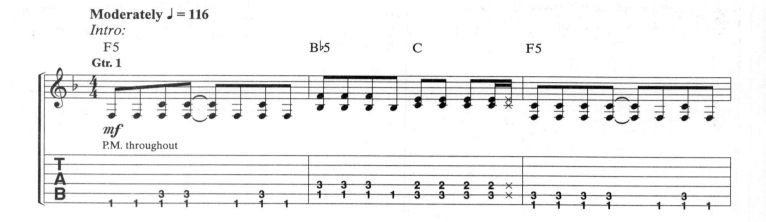

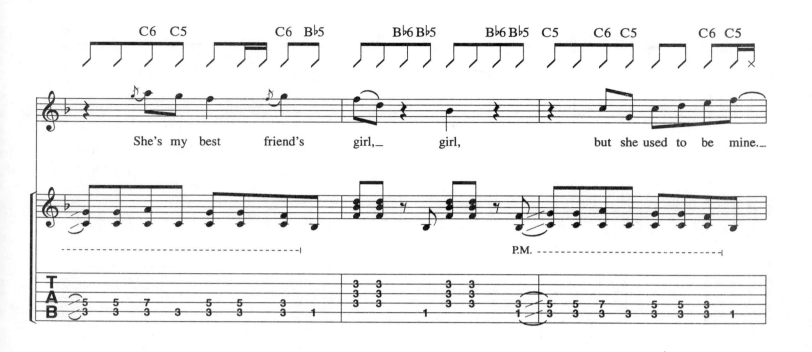

She's my best friend's girl,__ girl,__ but she used to be mine.__

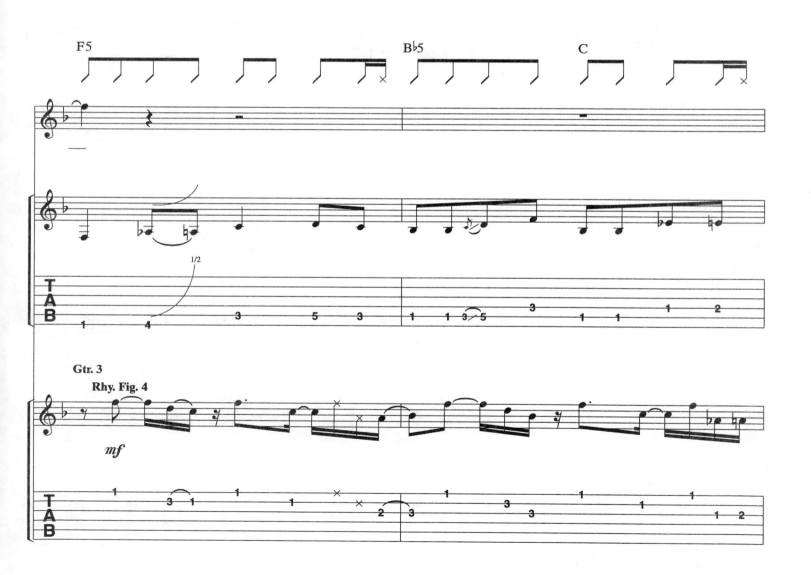

2. You've *got your*

nu - cle - ar boots_ and your drip - dried_ glove.
(3.) danc - in' down the street with your suede - blue_ eyes.

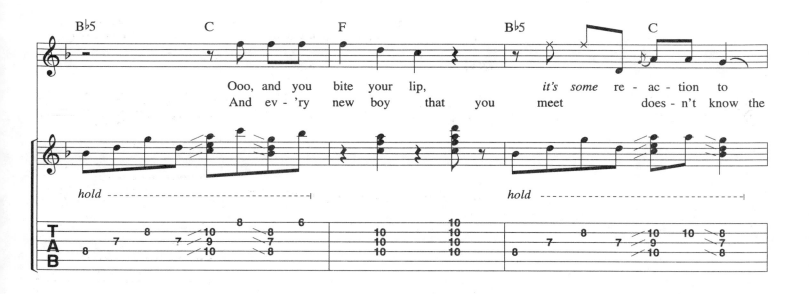

Ooo, and you bite your lip, *it's some* re - ac - tion to
And ev - 'ry new boy that you meet does - n't know the

Pre-Chorus:

w/Fill 1 *(Gtr. 2)*

w/**Rhy. Fig. 1** *(Gtr. 1)* & **Riff A** *(Gtr. 2) both simile*

love. When she's
real sur - prise. Here she comes a - gain.

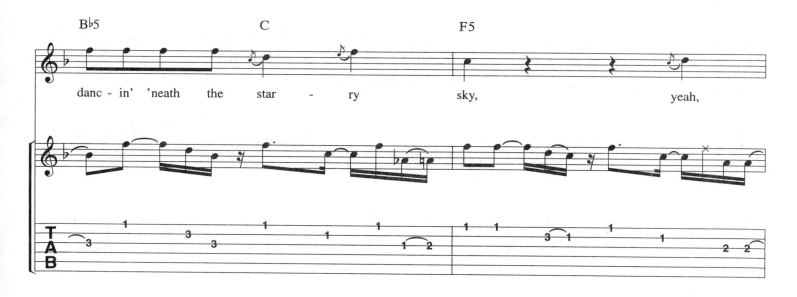

danc - in' 'neath the star - ry sky, yeah,

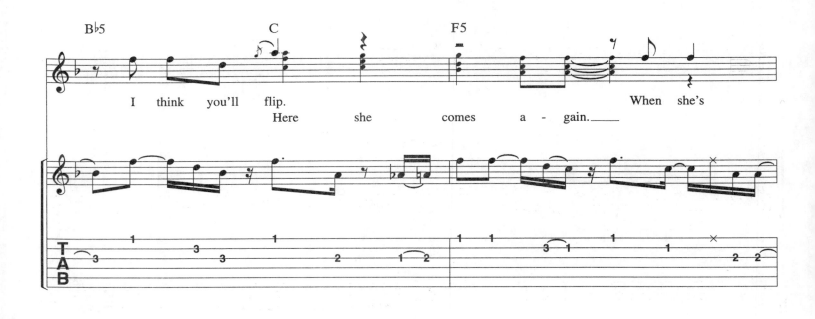

I think you'll flip.

Here she comes a-gain.____ When she's

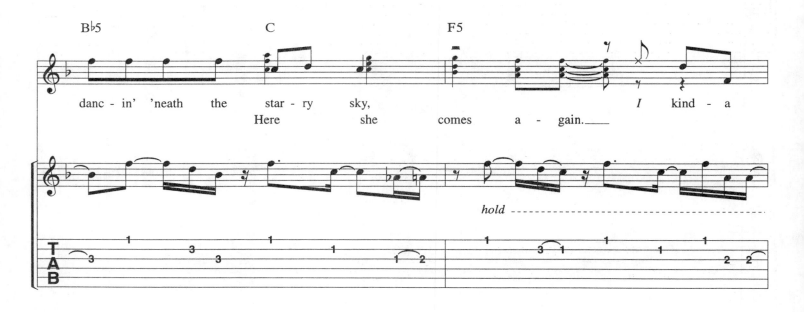

danc-in' 'neath the star-ry sky,

Here she comes a-gain.____ I kind-a

hold -

Chorus:
w/Rhy. Figs. 3 *(Gtr. 1)*
& 3A *(Gtr. 2) both simile*

like the way, I like the way she dips. She's my best friend's

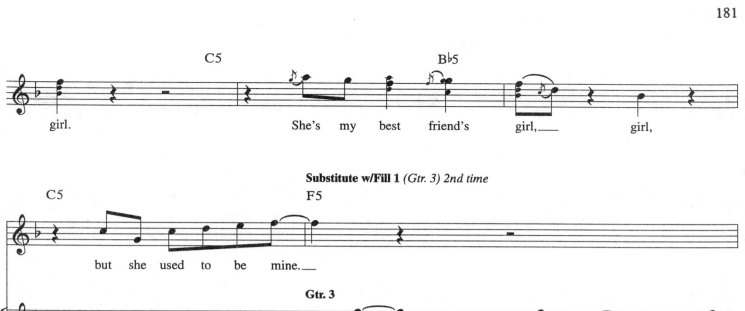

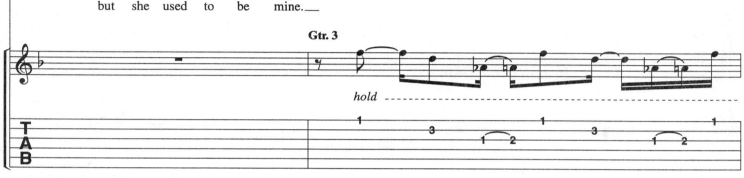

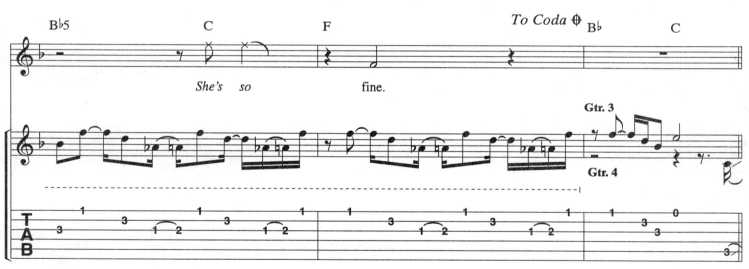

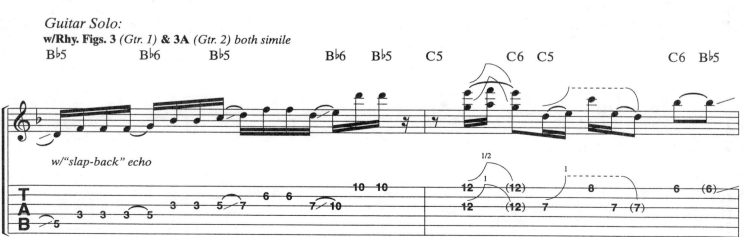

My Best Friend's Girl - 10 - 8

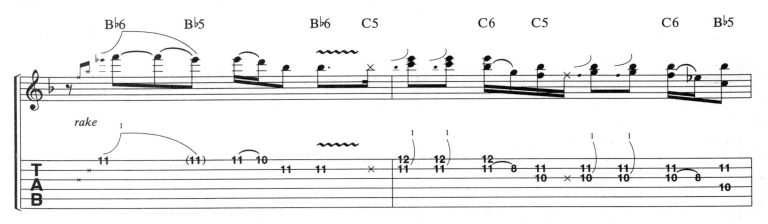

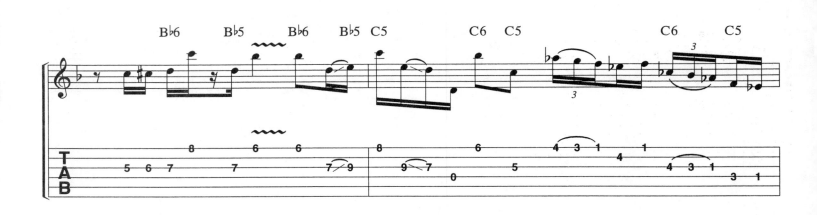

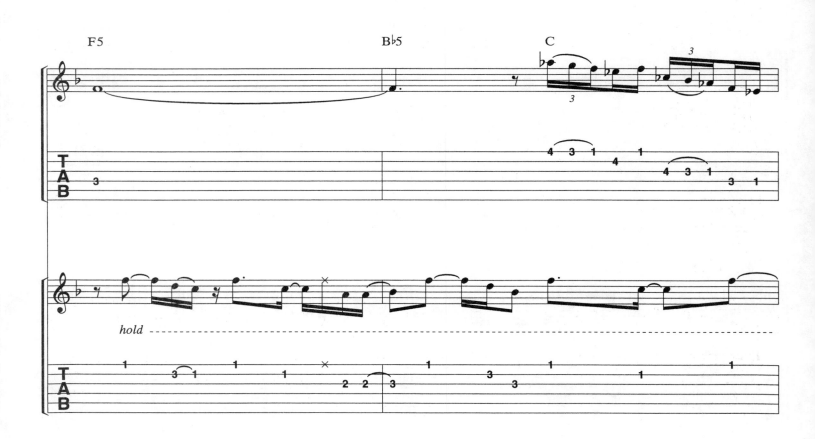

*w/Lead vocal ad lib. on repeats.

NEVER

Words and Music by HOLLY KNIGHT,
GENE BLOCH, ANN WILSON
and NANCY WILSON

*Chord symbols derived from combining gtr. and keybds. throughout.

1.3. Hey ba-by, I'm talk-in' to you; _ stop your-self and _ lis-ten.
2. *See additional lyrics*

Never – 7 – 2

Verse 2:
Hey baby, you know it's true.
Why you bother lying when you know
That you want it, too?
Don't you dare deny it.
Now, walk those legs right over here,
Give me what I'm dying for,
One chance; one love; hold me down, never let me go.
(To Chorus:)

ONE WAY OR ANOTHER

Elec. Gtr. 1 tuned to "drop D":
⑥ = D ③ = G
⑤ = A ② = B
④ = D ① = E

Words and Music by
DEBORAH HARRY and
NIGEL HARRISON

*2nd time only.

*Elec. Gtr. 3

*1st 2 measures during Verse 3 only:

One Way or Another - 5 - 1

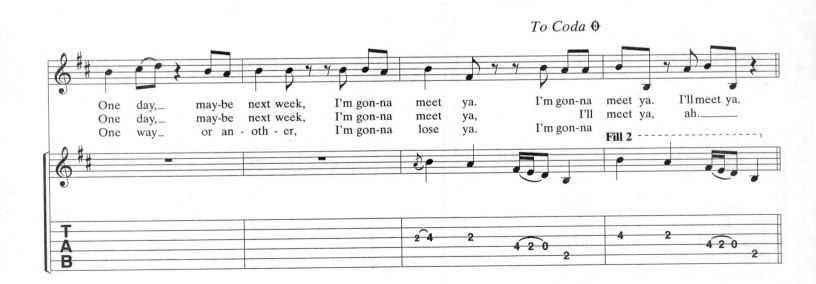

One Way or Another - 5 - 3

Coda

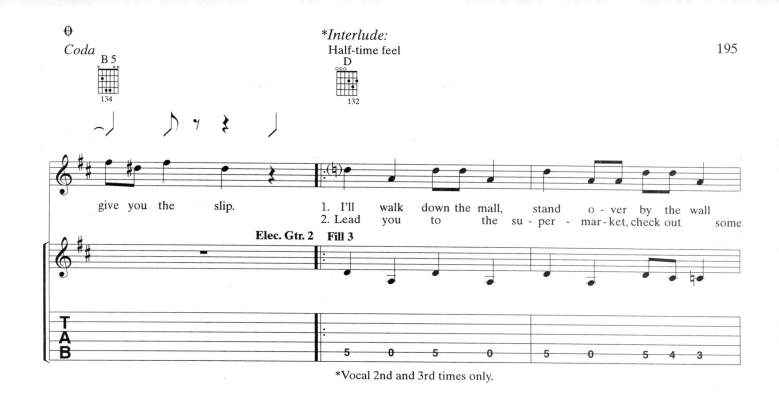

Vocal 2nd and 3rd times only.

Outro:
*end half-time feel
w/Fill 3 (Elec. Gtr. 2) simile*

Repeat and fade

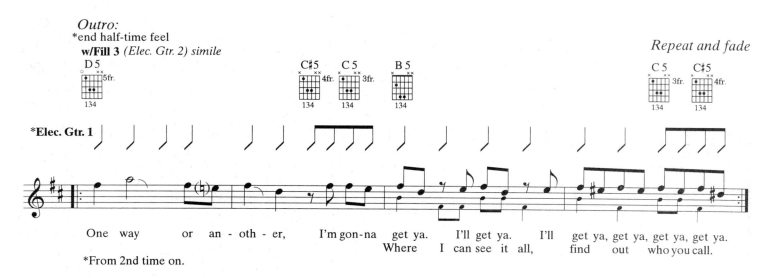

From 2nd time on.

One Way or Another - 5 - 5

NEW WORLD MAN

Words by
NEIL PEART

Music by
GEDDY LEE and ALEX LIFESON

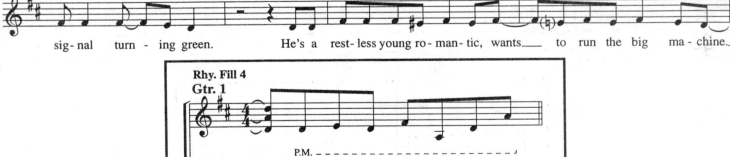

He's a 1. re - bel and a run - ner. He's a
2. *See additional lyrics*

sig - nal turn - ing green. He's a rest - less young ro - man - tic, wants___ to run the big ma - chine.

Learn - ing to catch the___ heat___ of the Third World man.

1. He's got___ to make___ his own___
2. *See additional lyrics*

Pre-Chorus 1 & 2:

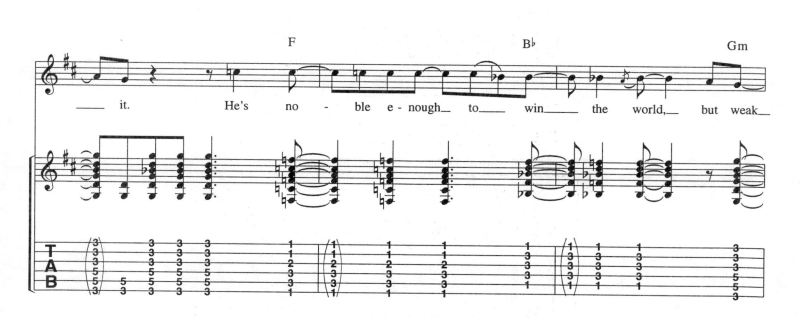

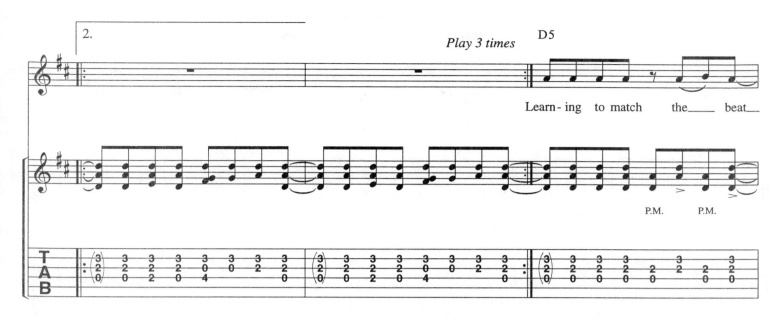

New World Man - 8 - 6

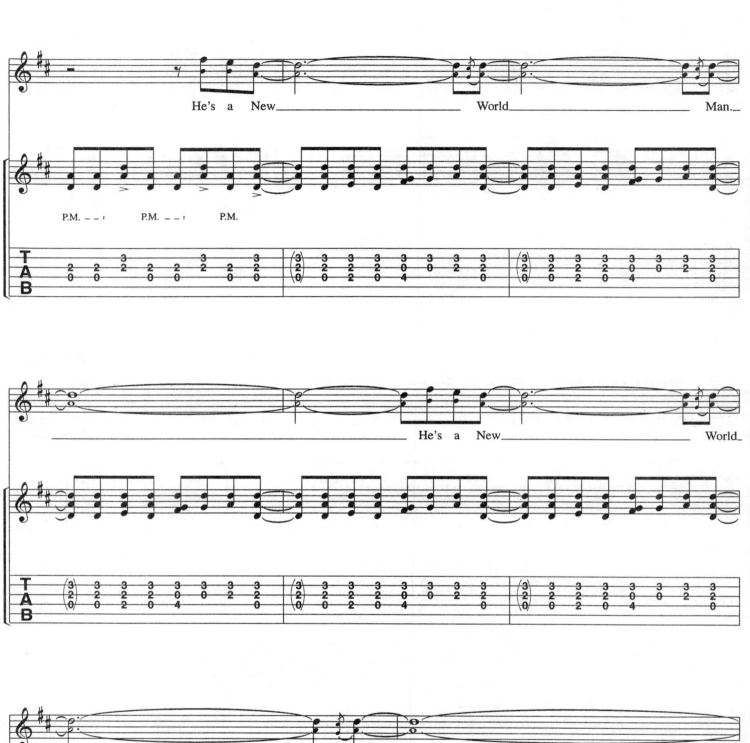

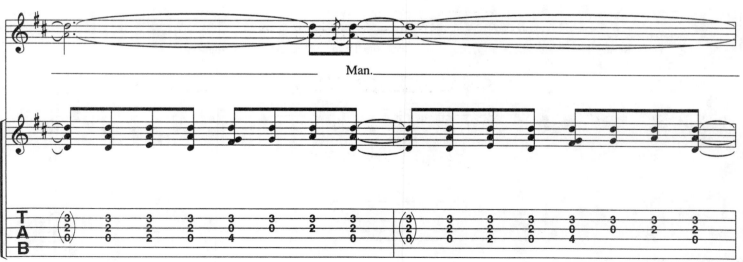

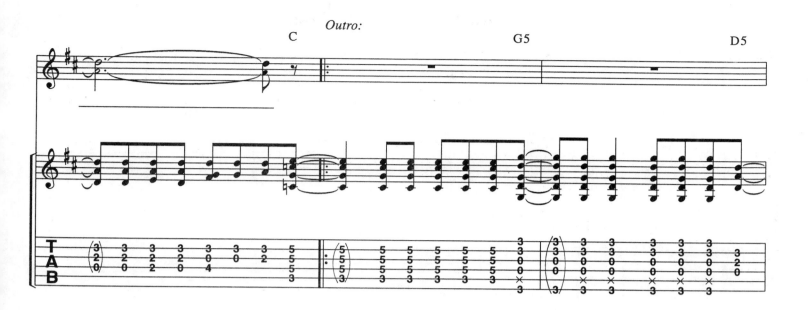

Verse 2:

He's a radio receiver, tuned to factories and farms.
He's a writer and arranger and a young boy bearing arms.
He's got a problem with his power, with weapons on patrol.
He's got to walk a fine line and keep his self-control.

Bridge 2:

Trying to save the day for the Old World man.
Trying to pave the way for the Third World man.

Interlude 2:

He's not concerned with yesterday.
He knows constant change is here today.

Pre-Chorus 2:

He's noble enough to know what's right,
But weak enough not to choose it.
He's wise enough to win the world,
But fool enough to lose it.

OPEN ARMS

Words and Music by
STEVE PERRY and JONATHAN CAIN

Intro:

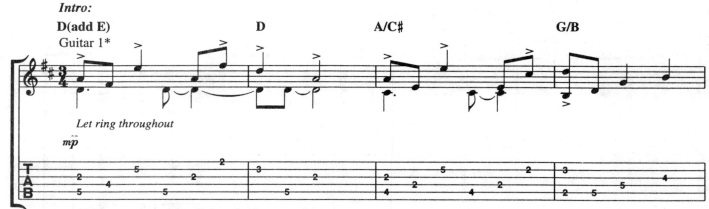

*Piano arranged for Guitar 1. (finger style)
Acoustic with capo at 2nd fret is recommended.*

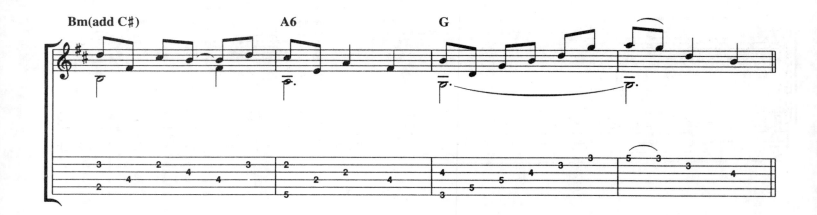

Verse 1:

1. Ly - ing ____ be - side ____ you, here in ____ the dark,

Rhythm Figure 1

Open Arms - 9 - 1

Pre-Chorus 1:

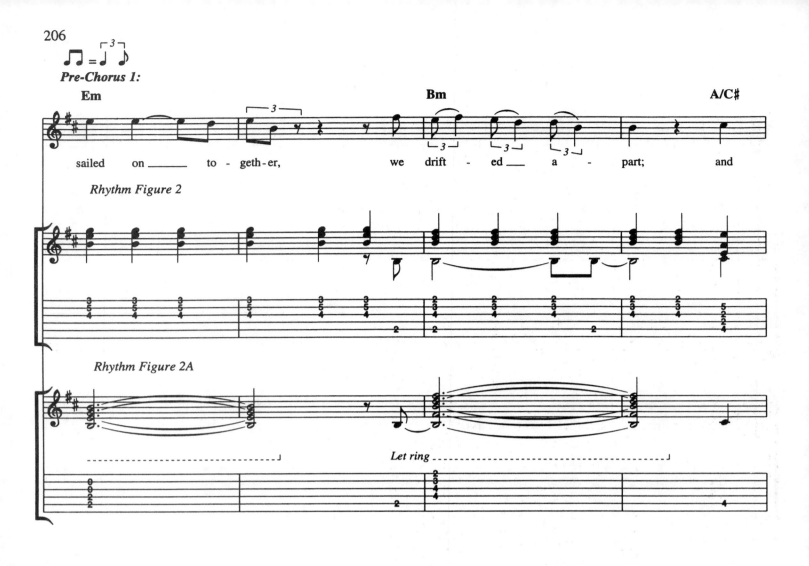

sailed on _____ to-geth-er, we drift - ed _____ a - part; and

Rhythm Figure 2

Rhythm Figure 2A

Let ring _____

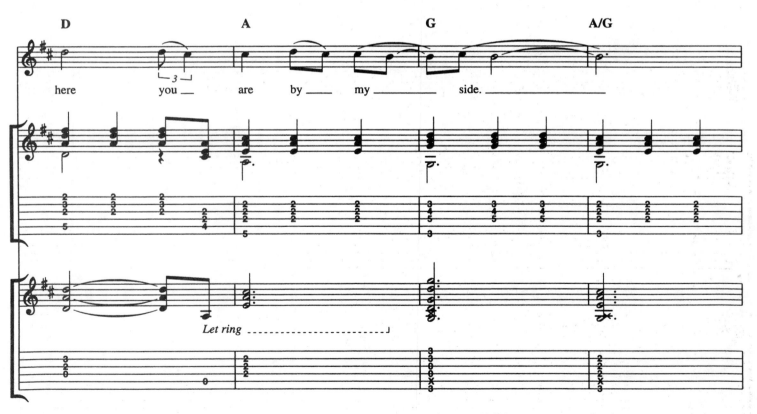

here you _____ are by _____ my _____ side. _____

Let ring _____

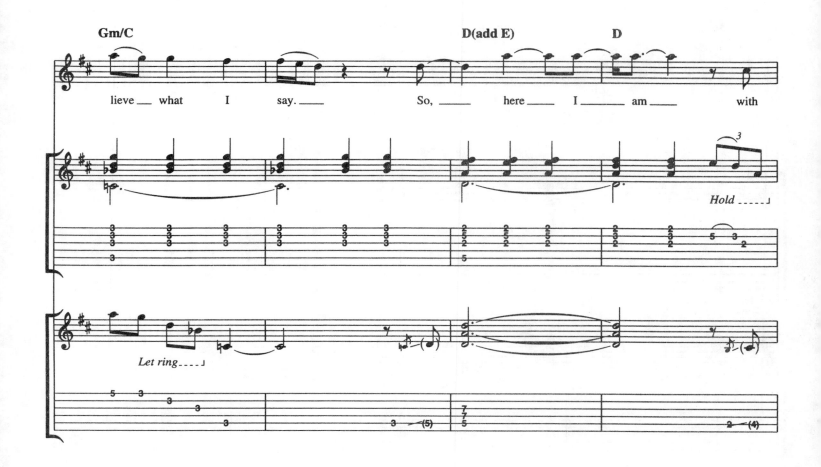

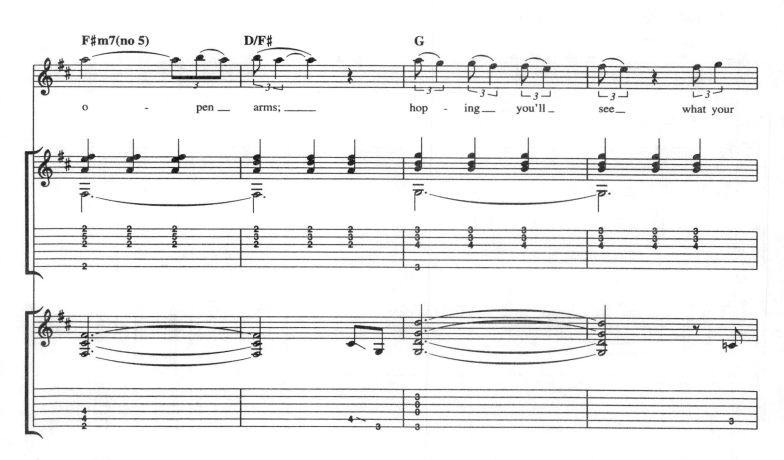

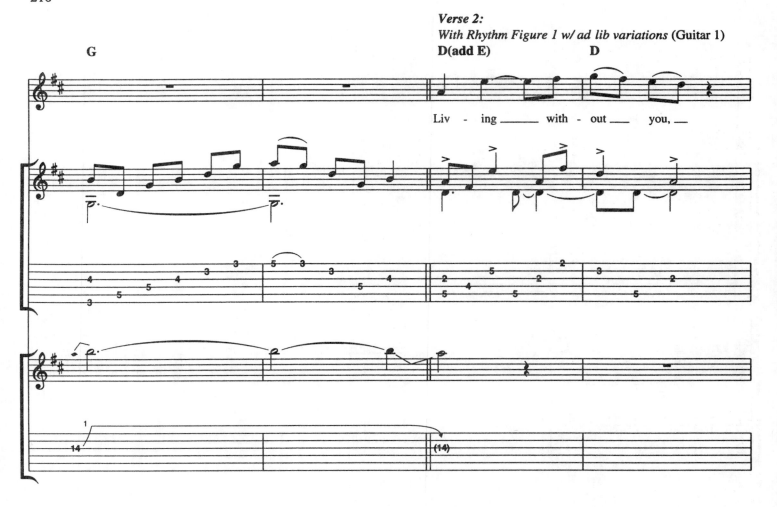

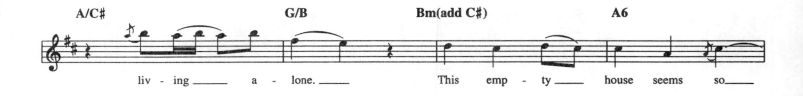

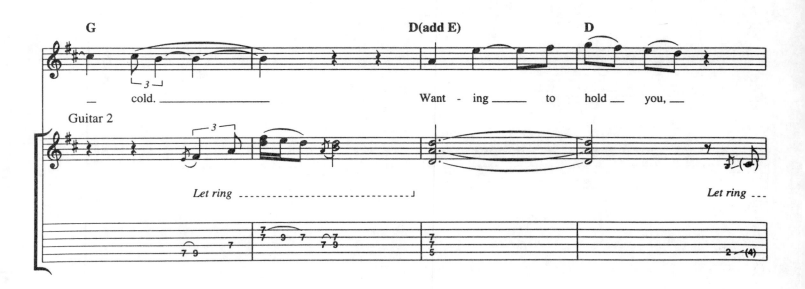

PSYCHO KILLER

Words and Music by
DAVID BYRNE, CHRIS FRANTZ
and MARTINA WEYMOUTH

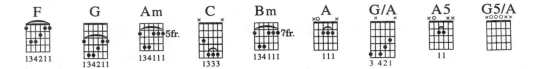

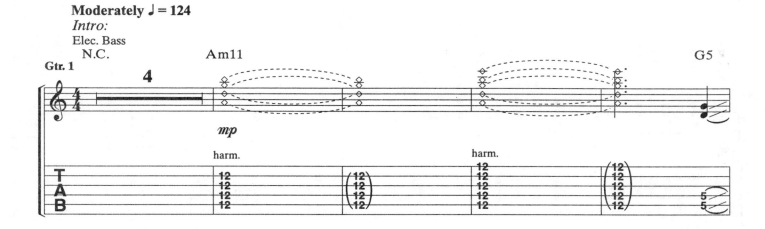

Psycho Killer - 9 - 1

Verse:

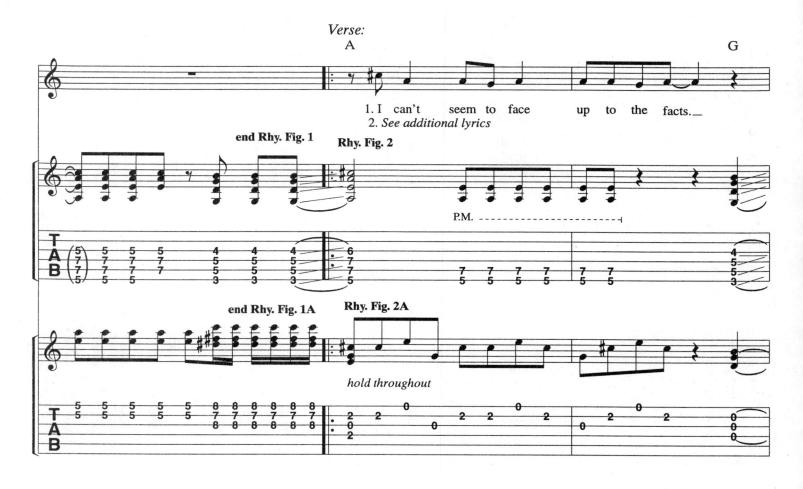

1. I can't seem to face up to the facts.__
2. *See additional lyrics*

I'm tense and nerv-ous, and I can't re-lax.__ I can't sleep 'cause my

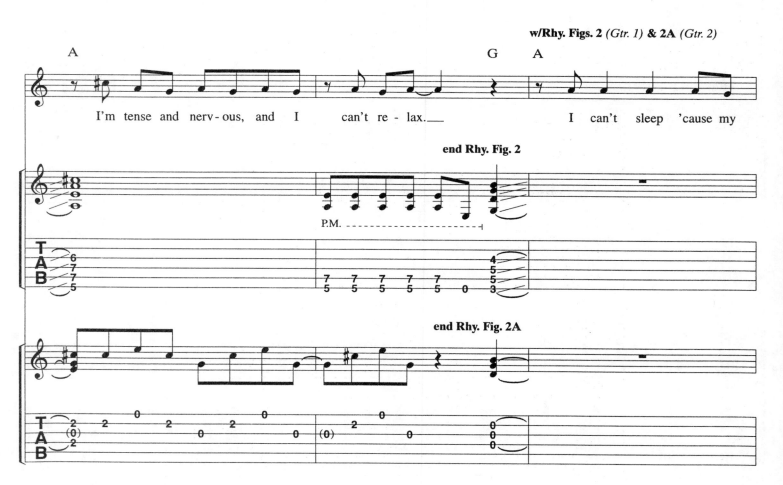

216

218

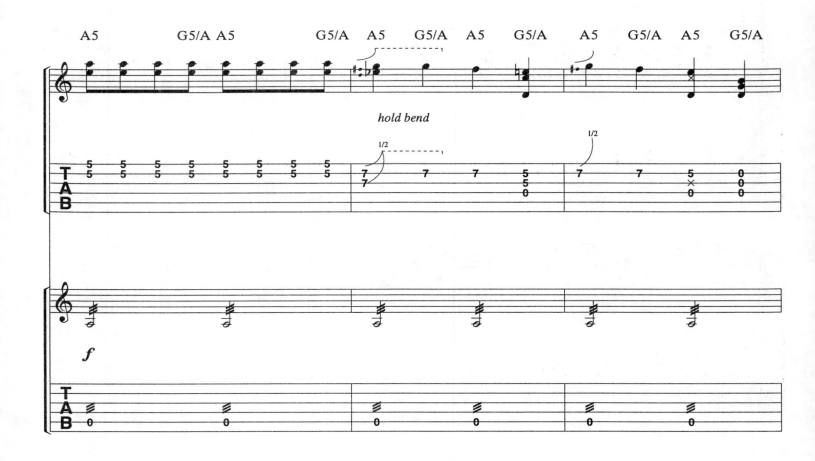

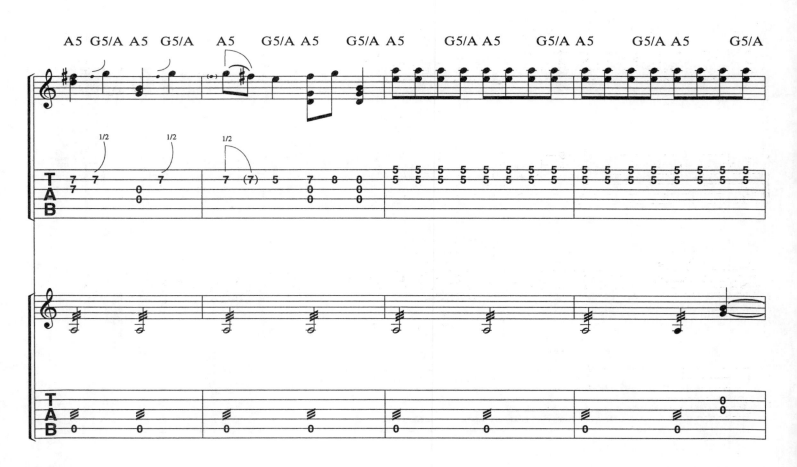

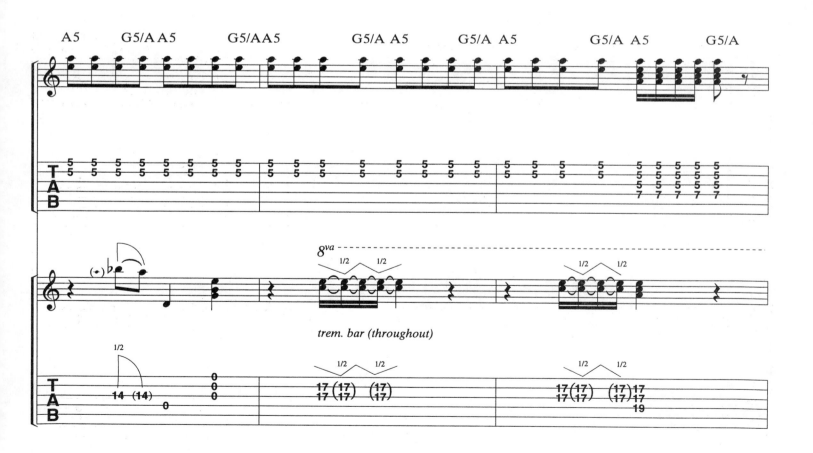

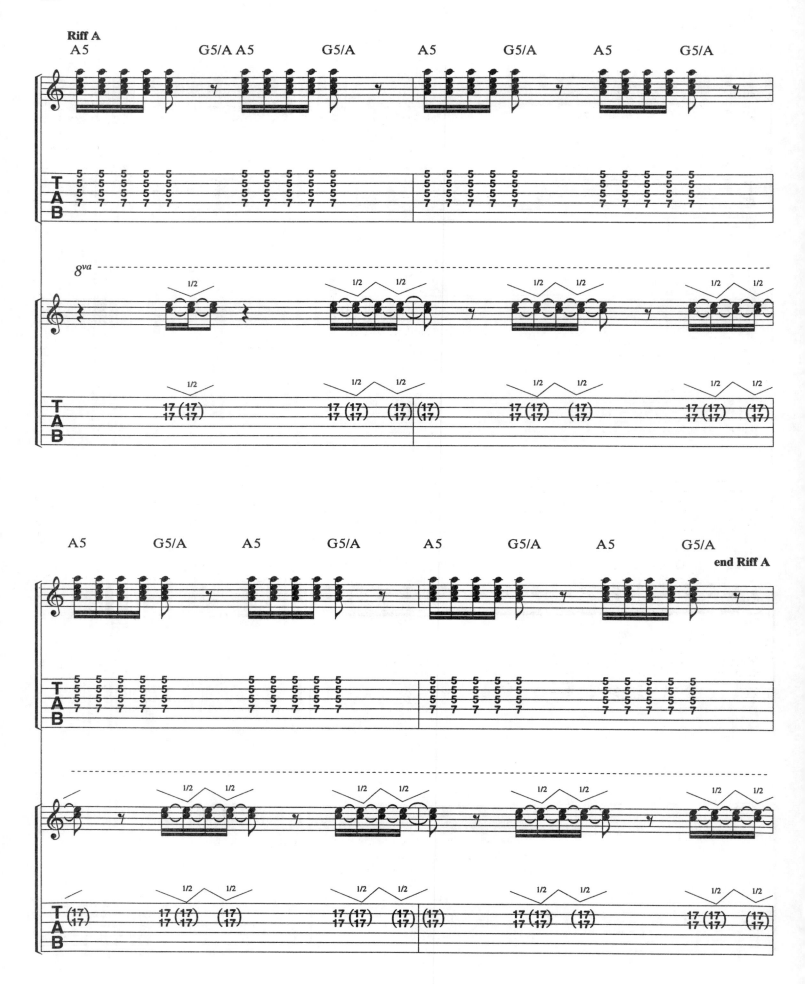

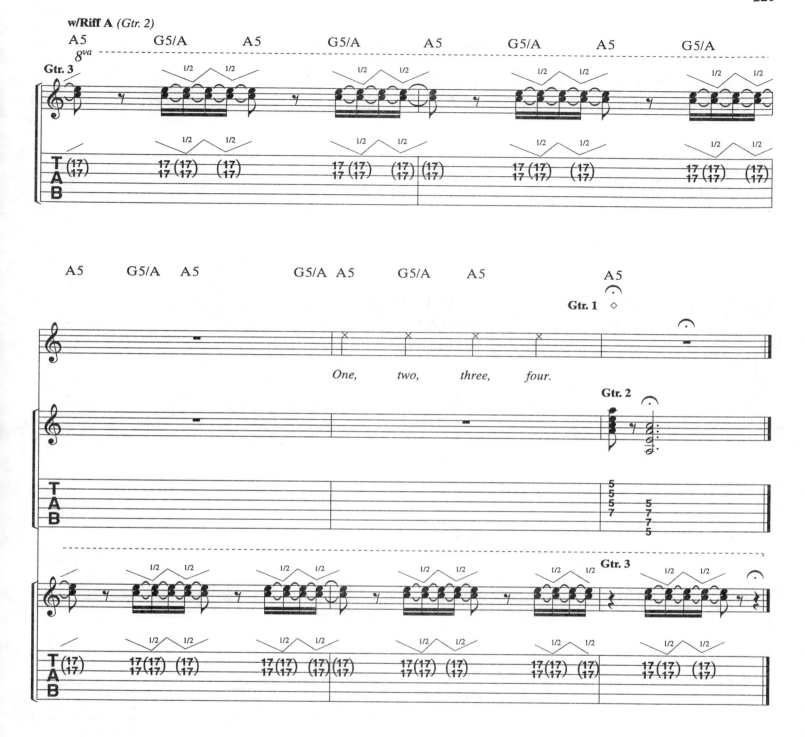

Verse 2:
You start a conversation, you can't even finish it.
You're talking a lot, but you're not saying anything.
When I have nothing to say, my lips are sealed.
Say something once, why say it again?
(To Chorus:)

PANAMA

Words and Music by
EDWARD VAN HALEN, ALEX VAN HALEN,
MICHAEL ANTHONY and DAVID LEE ROTH

Panama - 8 - 1

PHOTOGRAPH

**Words and Music by STEVE CLARK,
JOE ELLIOTT, R.J. LANGE,
RICK SAVAGE and PETE WILLIS**

Tune down ½ step:
⑥ = Eb ③ = Gb
⑤ = Ab ② = Bb
④ = Db ① = Eb

Moderate rock ♩ = 126

Intro:

(Approx. 2 sec.) w/chorus & delay

(Fade in) Oo.

Rhy. Fig. 1 *

*Doubled by another gtr.

Verse 1:
w/Rhy. Fig. 1 *(Gtr. 1)*

end Rhy. Fig. 1

I'm out-a luck, ___ out-a love. ___ Got a pho-to-graph, ___ pic-ture of ___

Photograph – 8 – 1

*Doubled by another gtr.

Guitar Solo:

PROWLER

**Words and Music by
STEVE HARRIS**

look - ing___ oh so pret - ty___
All their___ legs so and lash - es___

I've _____ just___

got to find___ my way._____

Well _____ you see me crawl - ing through___ the bush - es

with it o - pen wide.

What you

240

Prowler - 6 - 3

Got__ me__ talk - ing__ but feel__ like__ walk - ing__ a - round..

Prowler - 6 - 4

Guitar Strum - II

Got_____ me __ feel - ing__ my - self_____ and __

reel - ing_____ a __ Got_____ me __ talk - ing__ but

noth - ing's__ with me __ Got _____ me __

feel - ing__ my - self ___ and __ reel - ing _____ a -

RAG DOLL

Words and Music by
STEVEN TYLER, JOE PERRY,
JIM VALLANCE and HOLLY KNIGHT

*Elec. Gtr. 1 in open E tuning:
⑥ = E ③ = G♯
⑤ = B ② = B
④ = E ① = E

Moderately ♩ = 92

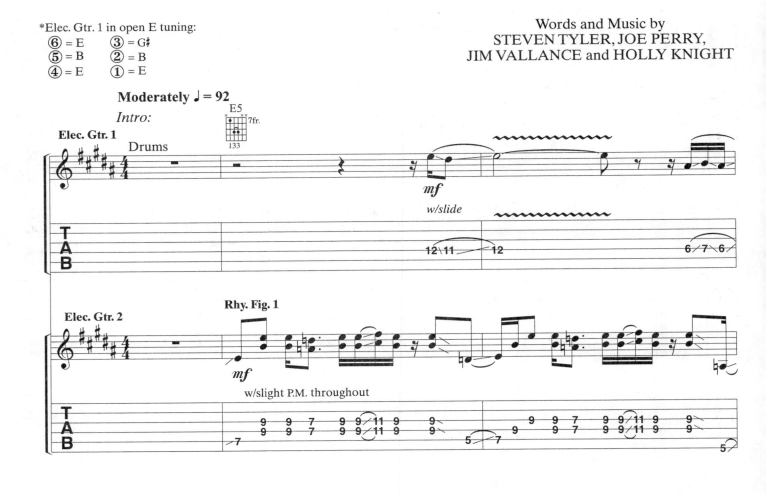

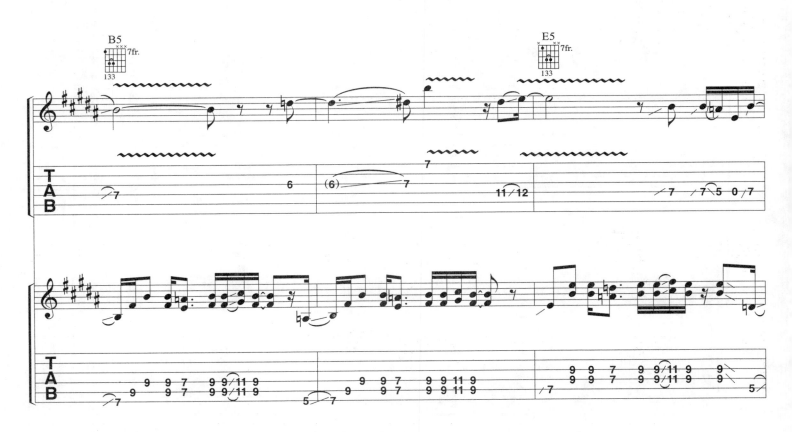

Guitar Solo:

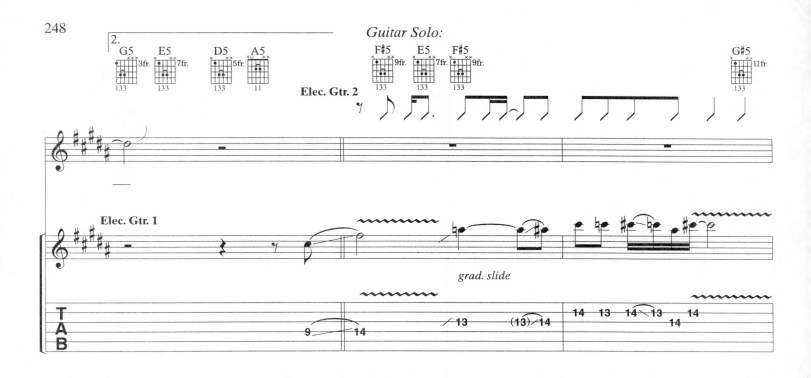

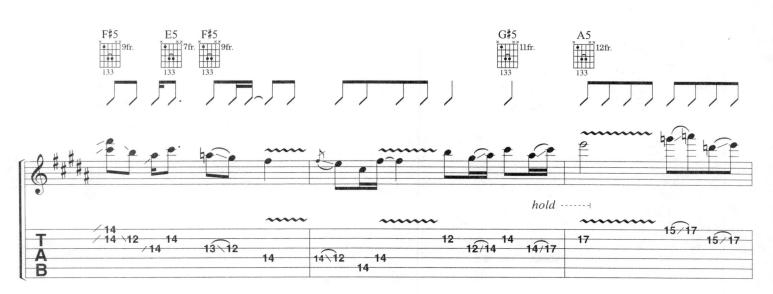

RAPTURE

Words and Music by
DEBORAH HARRY and
CHRIS STEIN

Rapture - 4 - 1

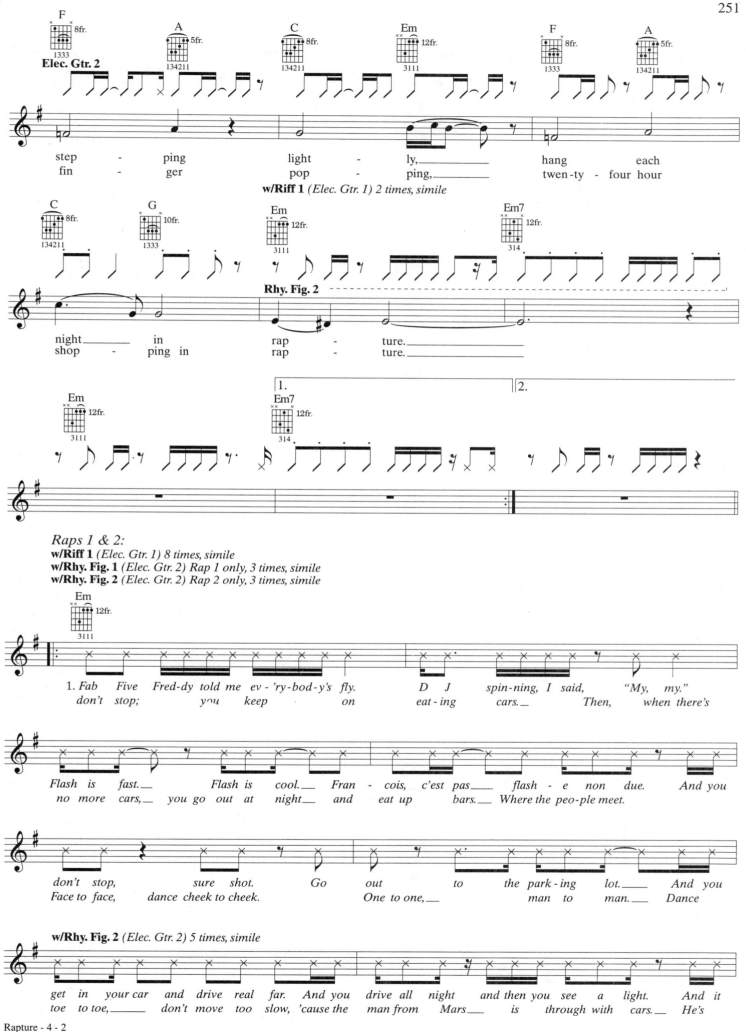

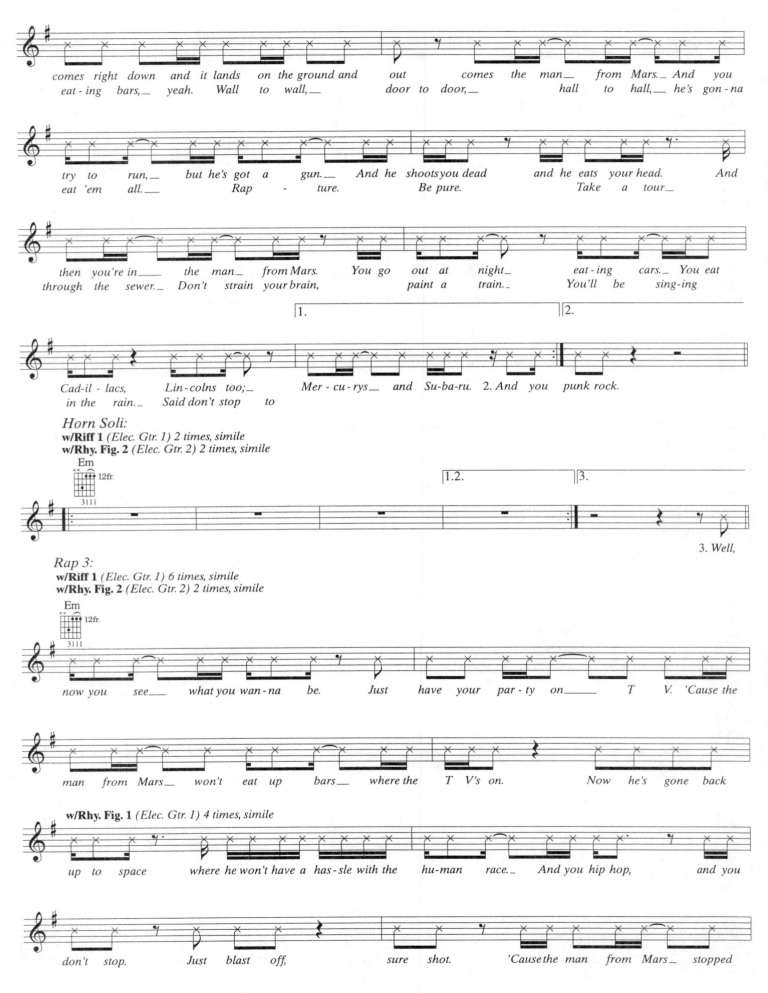

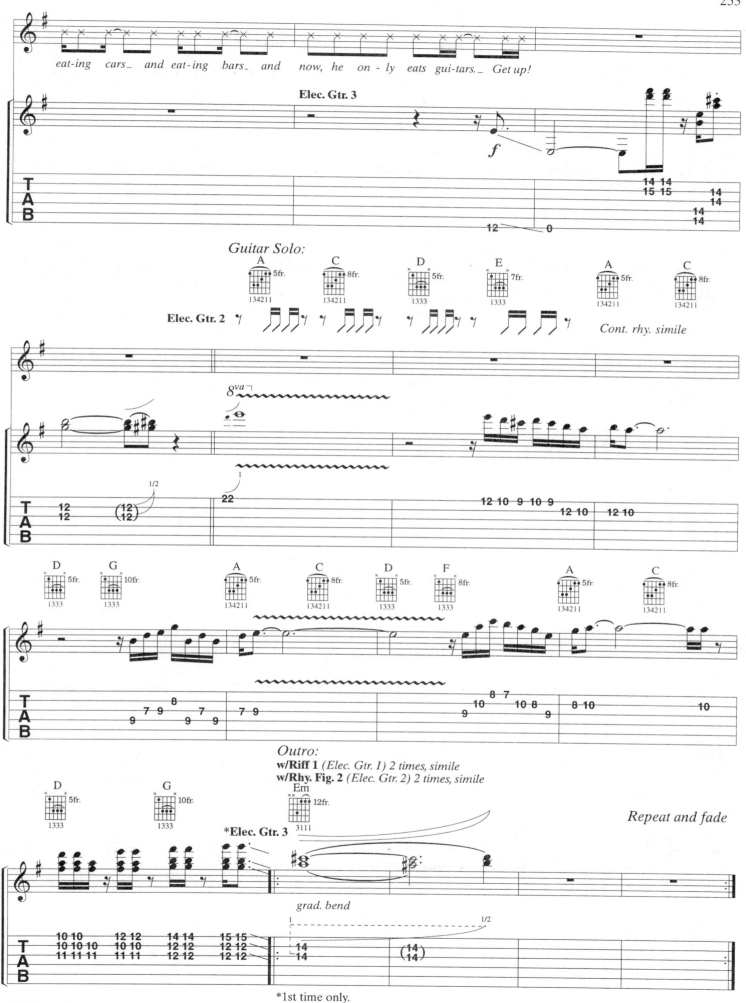

Rapture - 4 - 4

REBEL YELL

Words and Music by
BILLY IDOL and STEVE STEVENS

*Play upstem notes w/fingers and downstem w/pick.

w/Rhy. Fig. 2 *(Elec. Gtr. 3) simile*

Bm

In the mid-night hour,___ babe, "More, more, more."___

To Coda ⊕ | 1.

D/A   D/G   D5   A5

With a reb-el yell,___ "More, more, more,___ more, more,

| 2.

B5   A5 F♯5

w/fdbk.   pick sl.

more."___

(8va)

Elec. Gtr. 1

w/bar

fast vibrato ---slow vibrato------ pick sl.

8 1/2 harm.

Bridge:
w/Rhy. Fig. 1 *(Elec. Gtr. 3) 2 times, simile*

G5   F♯5   E5/F♯   E5   Em7   E5

1. A-he___ lives in-a his own heav-en.___
2. Well, he's out all night to col-lect a fare.___

| 1.

G5   F♯5   E5/F♯   E5   Em7   E5

He likes it "to go" from the Sev-en E-lev-en.___
Just as long, just as long's it don't mess

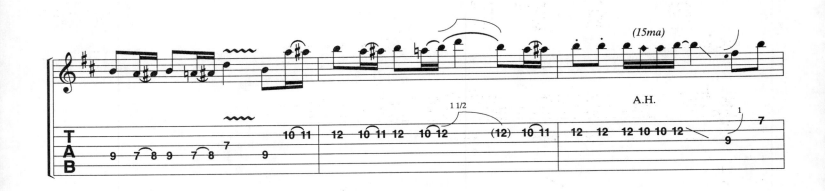

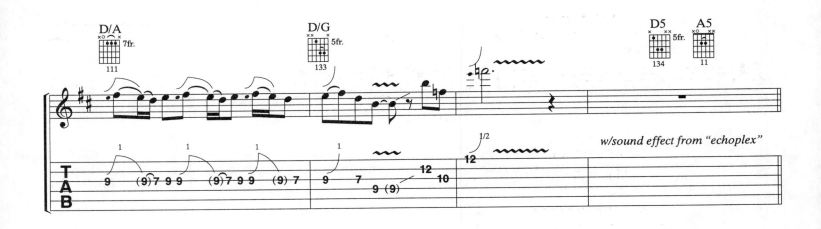

Interlude:

Drums

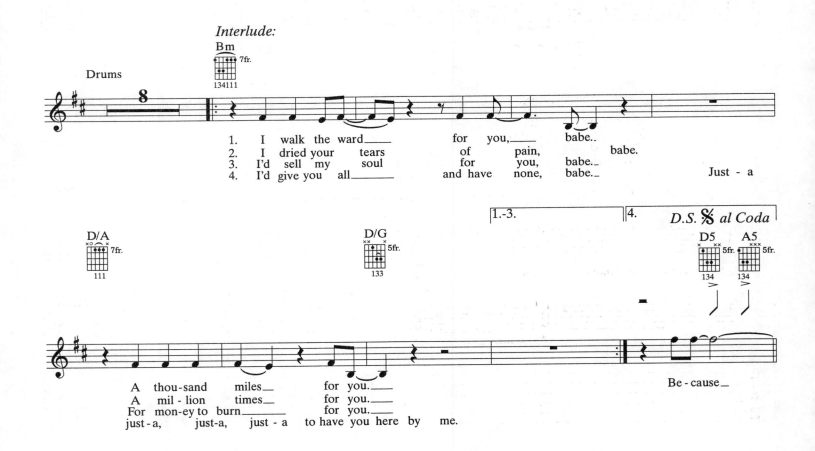

1. I walk the ward_____ for you,_____ babe.
2. I dried your tears of pain, babe.
3. I'd sell my soul for you, babe.
4. I'd give you all_____ and have none, babe._____ Just - a

1.-3.　　4.　D.S. 𝄋 al Coda

A thou-sand miles_____ for you._____
A mil - lion times_____ for you._____
For mon-ey to burn_____ for you._____
just - a,　just-a,　just - a to have you here by me.

Be - cause_____

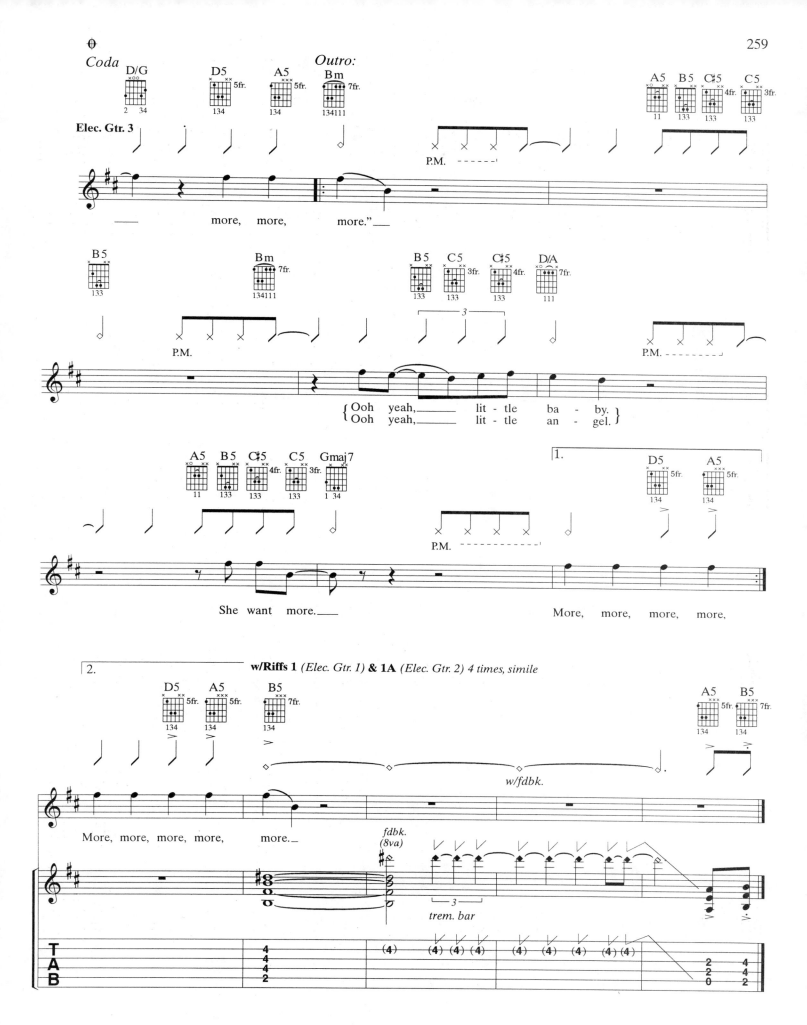

REMEMBER TOMORROW

Words and Music by
STEVE HARRIS and PAUL DI'ANNO

(Let low "E" note ring through)

Guitar Pattern - A

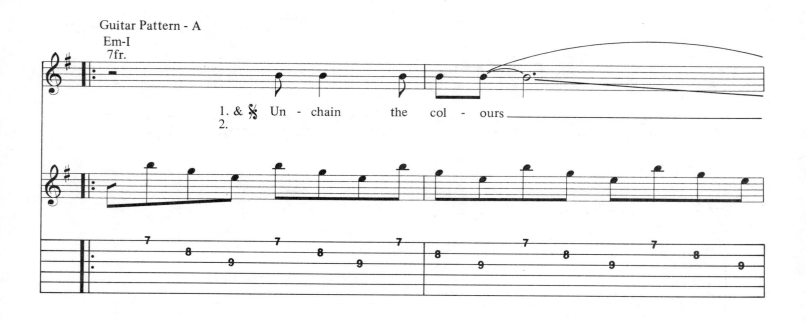

1. & 𝄋 Un - chain the col - ours
2.

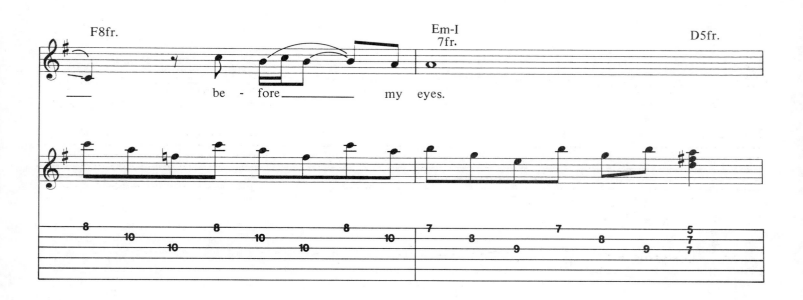

be - fore ___ my eyes.

Guitar Pattern - A

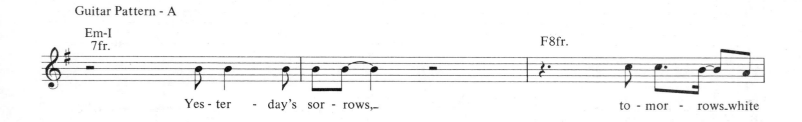

Yes - ter - day's sor - rows,___ to - mor - rows_white

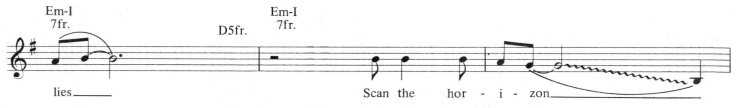

lies___ Scan the hor - i - zon___

2. Tears for rememberance
   and tears for joy,
   Tears for somebody
   and this lonely boy,
   Out in the madness
   the all seeing eye,
   Flickers above us
   to light up the sky.

SHARP DRESSED MAN

Words and Music by
BILLY GIBBONS, DUSTY HILL
and FRANK BEARD

Sharp Dressed Man - 3 - 1

Verse 2:
Gold watch, diamond ring,
I ain't missin' not a single thing.
Cuff links, stick pin,
When I step out I'm gonna do you in.
They come runnin' just as fast as they can,
'Cause every girl crazy 'bout a sharp dressed man.
(To Guitar Solo:)

Verse 3:
Top coat, top hat,
I don't worry 'cause my wallet's fat.
Black shades, white gloves,
Lookin' sharp and lookin' for love.
They come runnin' just as fast as they can,
'Cause every girl crazy 'bout a sharp dressed man.
(To Coda)

ROSANNA

Words and Music by
DAVID PAICH

*Piano arr. for gtr. throughout.

Rosanna - 10 - 1

Verse:
w/Fill 1 *(Gtr. 1) 2 times*
w/Rhy. Fig. 1 *(Gtr. 2)*

1. All I wan-na do when I wake up in the morn-ing is see your eyes.___ Ro -
2. *See additional lyrics*

san - na,___ Ro - san - na,___ nev - er thought that a girl like you___ could ev - er

care for me.___ Ro - san - na.___

All I wan-na do in the mid-dle of the eve-'ning is

Chorus:
w/Fill 2 *(Gtr. 1) 4 times*

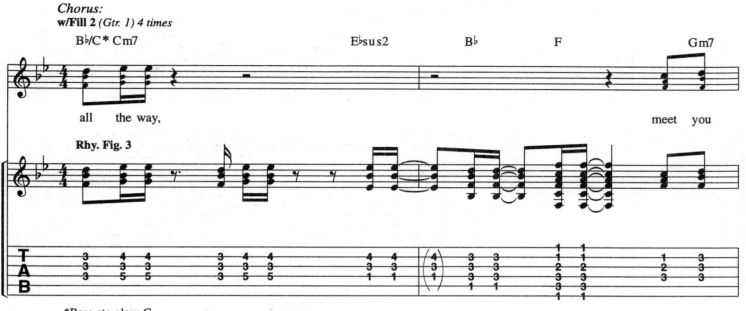

*Bass gtr. plays C.

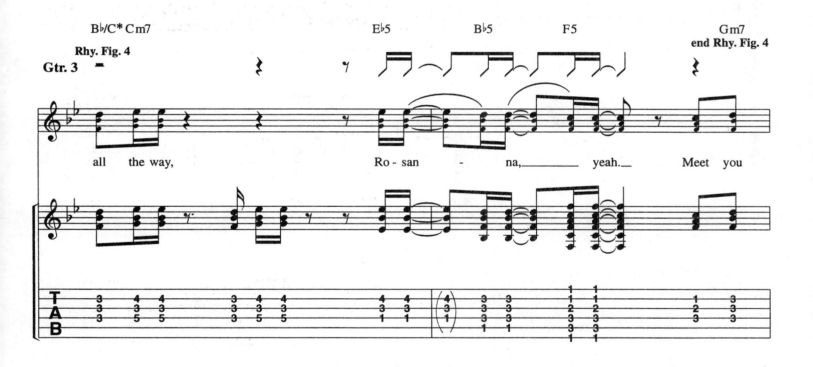

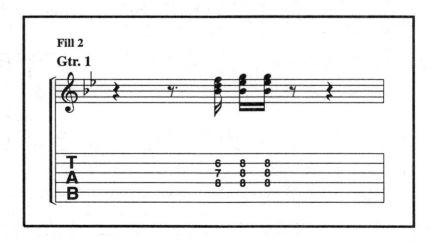

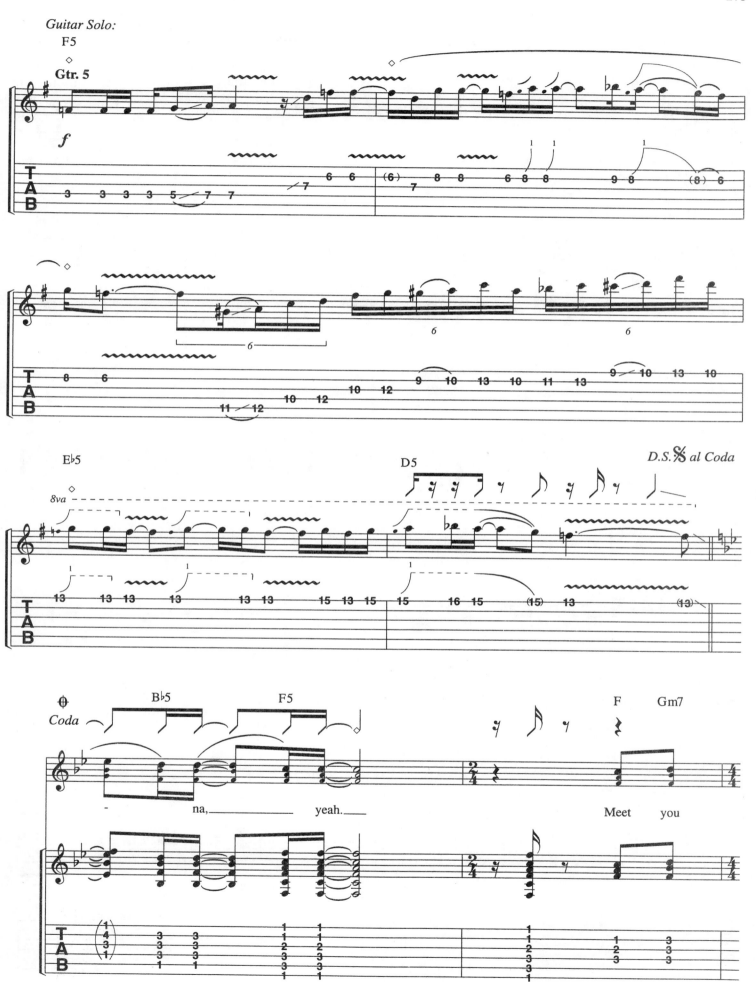

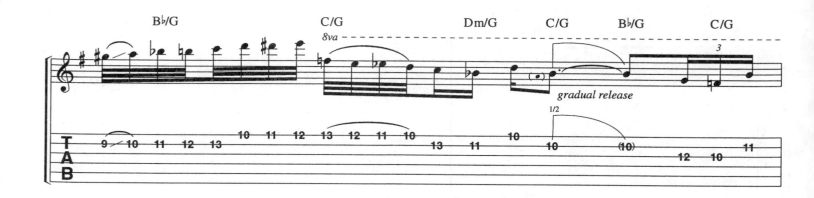

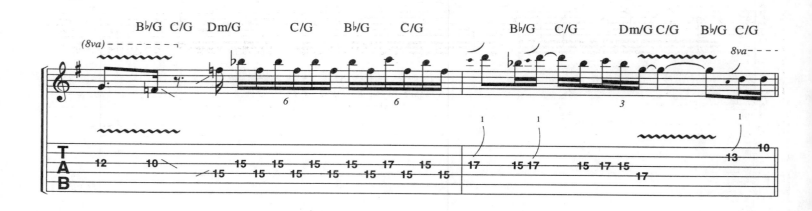

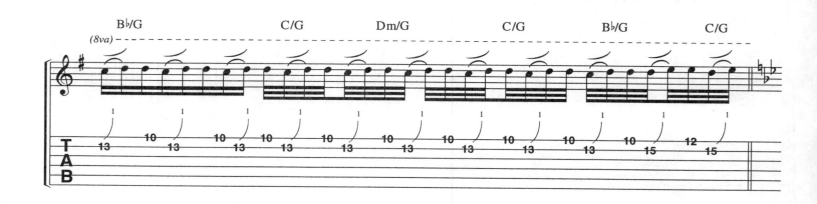

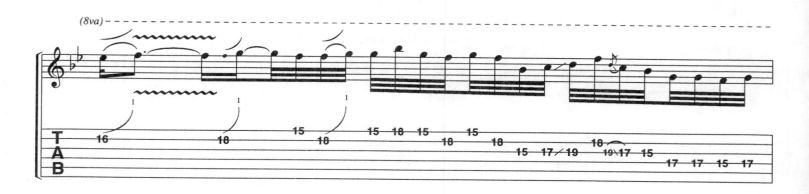

276

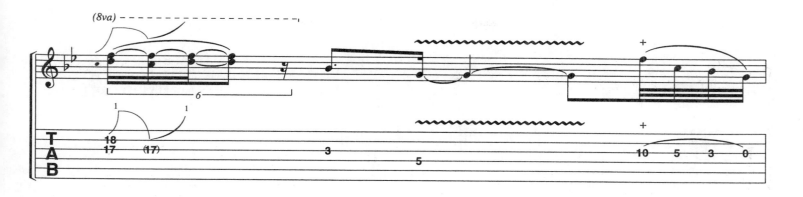

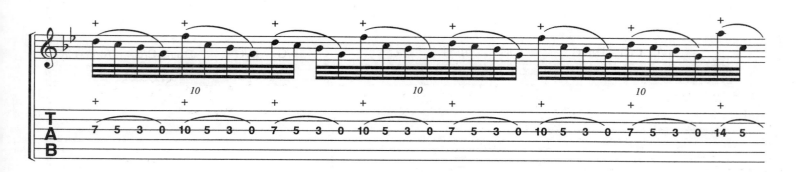

Fade

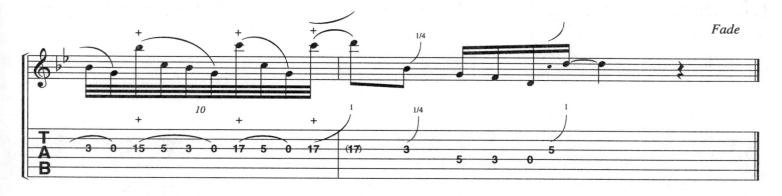

Verse 2:
I can see your face still shining
Through the window on the other side,
Rosanna, Rosanna.
I didn't know that a girl like
You could make me feel so sad, Rosanna.
All I want to tell you is now
You'll never, ever have to compromise,
Rosanna, Rosanna.
I never thought that losin' you
Could ever hurt so bad.
(To Pre-Chorus:)

RUNNIN' WITH THE DEVIL

Words and Music by
EDWARD VAN HALEN, ALEX VAN HALEN,
MICHAEL ANTHONY and DAVID LEE ROTH

Runnin' With the Devil - 6 - 1

Runnin' With the Devil - 6 - 4

283

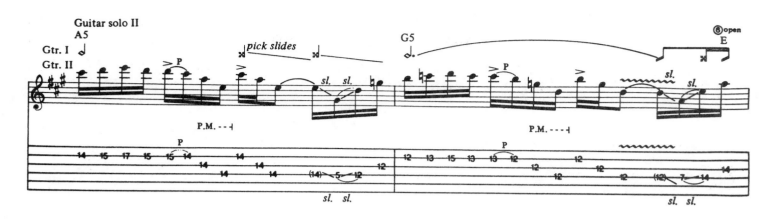

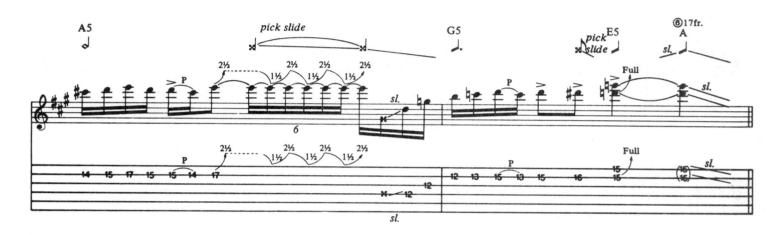

Runnin' With the Devil - 6 - 6

SANCTUARY

Words and Music by
STEVE HARRIS, PAUL DI'ANNO
and DAVE MURRAY

Sanctuary - 4 - 1

(to 2nd end on D.S.)

Play four times

1.2.3.

4.

I know you'd have gone in - sane if you saw what I saw

so now I've got to look for

sanc - tu - ar - y from the law.

Guitar Lick: A
D no 3rd

Guitar Lick: B
D no 3rd

D.S. al Coda

3. So you

Coda

Guitar Lick: B
D no 3rd

1.

2.

2. I met up with a 'slinger last night to keep me alive.
He spends all his money on gambling and guns to survive.

3. I can laugh at the wind, I can howl at the rain.
Down in the Canyon or out in the plain.

SHEENA IS A PUNK ROCKER

Words and Music by JEFFREY HYMAN, JOHN CUMMINGS,
DOUGLAS COLVIN and THOMAS ERDELYI

Fast punk rock ♩ = 185

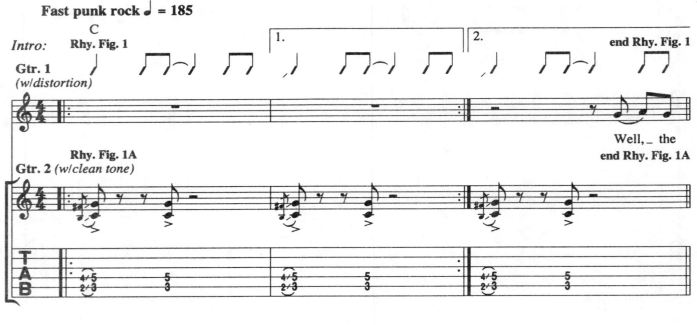

kids   are   all   hyped   up   and   read-y   to   go   they're read-y   to   go ___ now! *They*

got   their   surf   and then   they're   go-in'   to   the   dis - co - thèque - a - go - go.

Sheena Is a Punk Rocker - 3 - 1

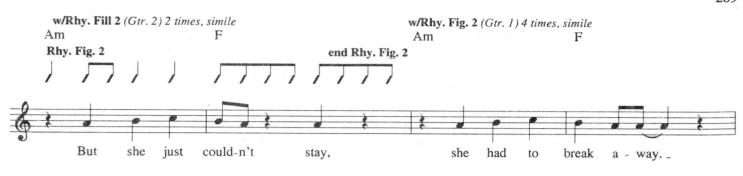

But she just could-n't stay, she had to break a-way.

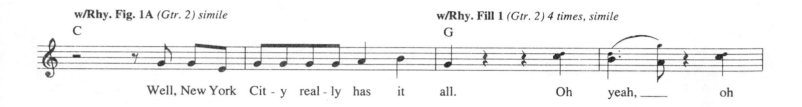

Well, New York Cit-y real-ly has it all. Oh yeah, ___ oh

Chorus:

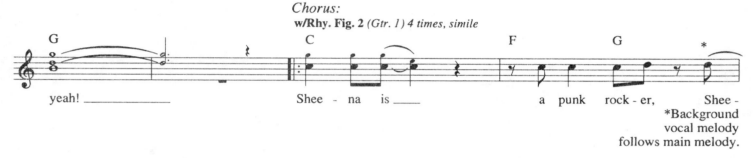

yeah! _____ Shee - na is ___ a punk rock-er, Shee -

*Background
vocal melody
follows main melody.

- na ___ is a punk rock-er, Shee - na is ___ a punk rock-er now! _

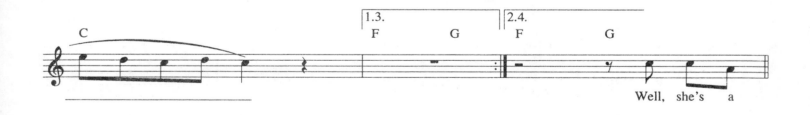

Well, she's a

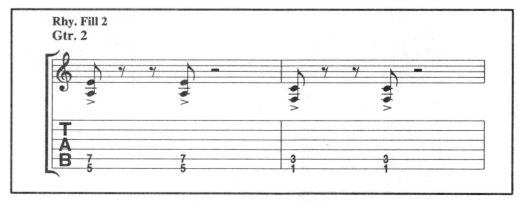

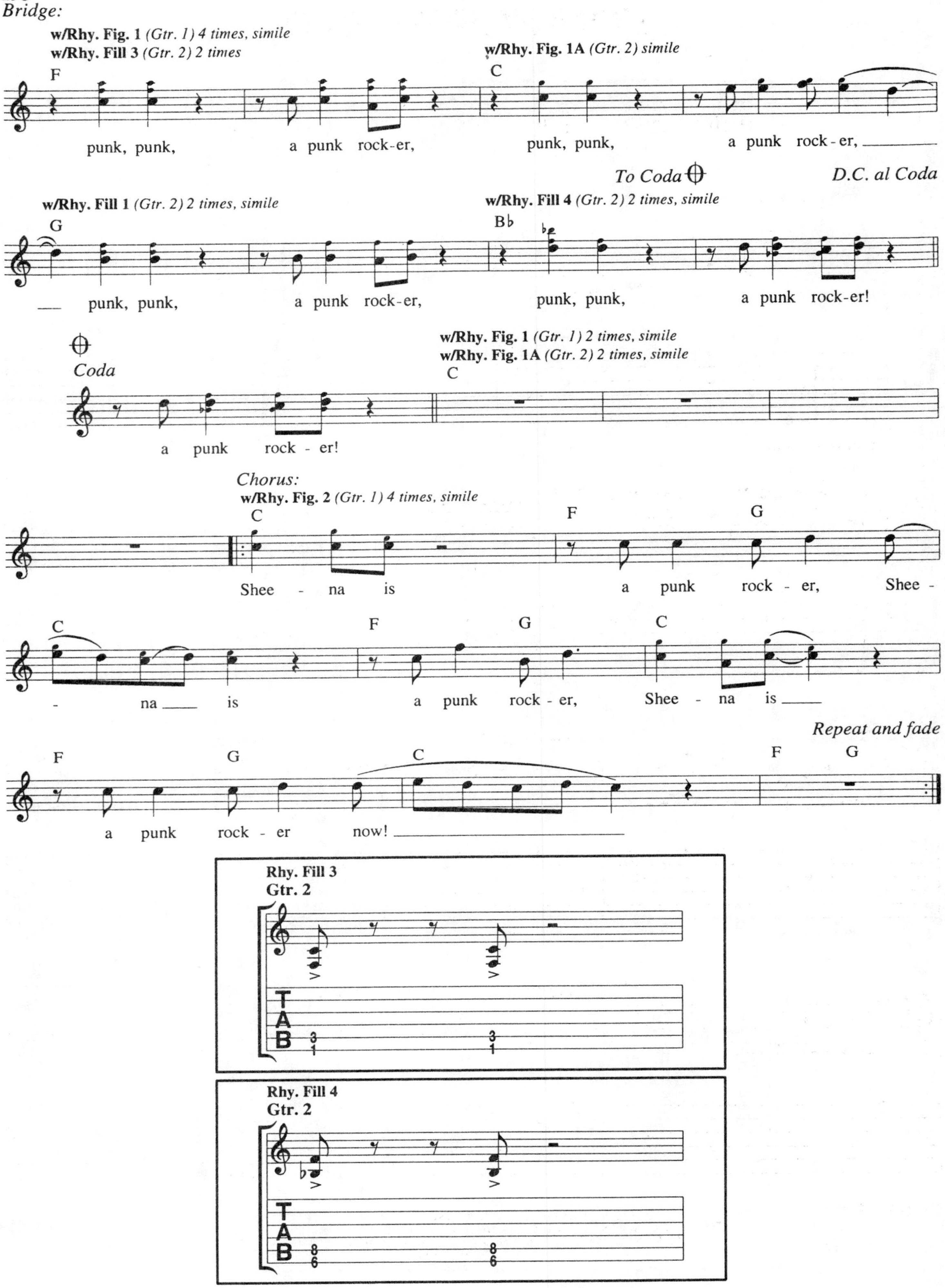

290

Bridge:

Sheena Is a Punk Rocker - 3 - 3

STRANGE WORLD

Words and Music by
STEVE HARRIS

Guittar Pattern - I

The on - ly place where you can dream liv - ing here is not what it seems.

Guittar Pattern - I

1. Ship of white light in the sky no - bod - y there to reas - on why
2nd verse
here I am, I'm not real - ly there. smil - ing fa - ces

2. Stalks of light come from the ground
   When I cry there isn't a sound
   All my feelings cannot be held
   I'm happy in my new strange world.
   Shades of green grasses twine,
   girls drinking plasma wine.
   A look at love, a dream unfolds
   living here, you'll never grow old.

THESE DREAMS

Words and Music by
BERNIE TAUPIN and MARTIN PAGE

These Dreams – 3 – 2

Verse 3:
Is it cloak and dagger?
Could it be spring or fall?
I walk without a cut through a stained glass wall.
Weaker in my eyesight, the candle in my grip.
And words that have no form
Are falling from my lips.
(To Chorus:)

Verse 4:
The sweetest song is silence that I've ever heard.
Funny how your feet in dreams never touch the earth.
In a wood full of princes, freedom is a kiss.
But the prince hides his face from the dreams in the mist.
(To Chorus:)

UNSKINNY BOP

Words and Music by
B. MICHAELS, B. DALL,
C.C. DEVILLE and R. ROCKETT

1. What's got you so jum-py,
2. *See additional lyrics*

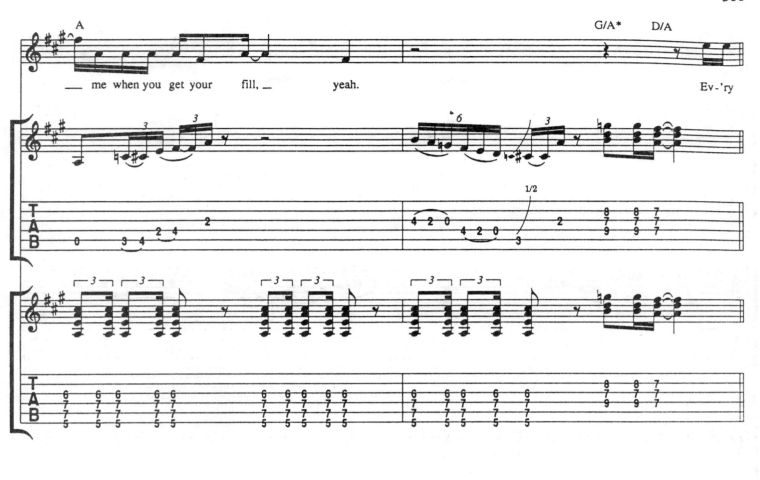

me when you get your fill, — yeah.

Ev-'ry

Pre-Chorus:

time I touch you, you get hot, — I wan-na make love, you nev - er stop, —

Gtr. 3

Gtr. 1

Unskinny Bop – 9 – 3

Unskinny Bop – 9 – 5

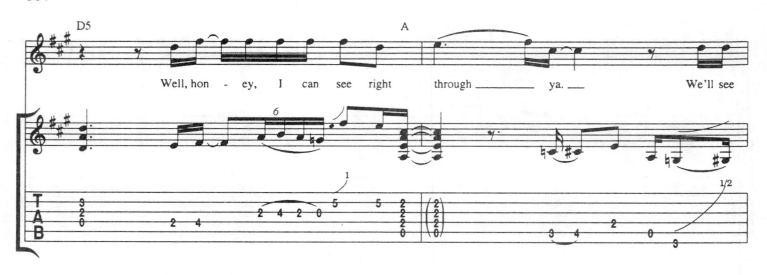

Well, hon - ey, I can see right through _____ ya. ___ We'll see

who's rid - ing who at the end of the race? _

Guitar Solo:

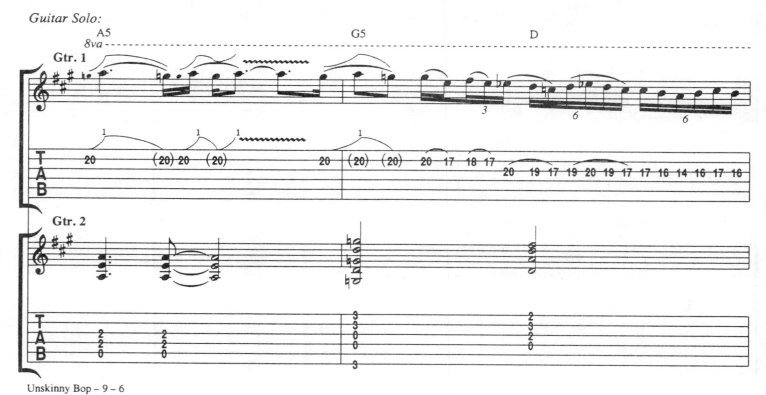

Chorus:

Un - skin-ny bop ___ just blows me a - way, ___ yeah. Un - skin-ny bop ___ bop,

all night and day. ___ Un - skin-ny bop, ___ bop, bop, ___ bop, she ___ just love to play. ___

*Repeat & fade

Come up for air, you pull me to the floor. ___

*Ad lib. lead gtr.
on repeats

Verse 2:

You look at me so funny,
Love bite got you acting oh so strange.
You got too many bees in your honey.
Am I just another word in your page?
Yeah, yeah.

(To Pre-Chorus:)

TOM SAWYER

Words by
PYE DUBOIS and NEIL PEART

Music by
GEDDY LEE and ALEX LIFESON

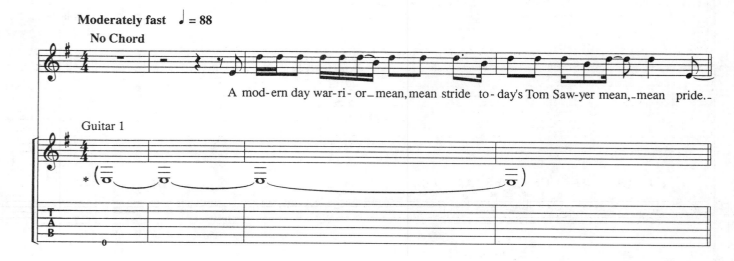

Moderately fast ♩ = 88

No Chord

A mod-ern day war-ri-or—mean, mean stride to-day's Tom Saw-yer mean,—mean pride.—

Guitar 1

* (Bass and flanged keyboard Intro.)

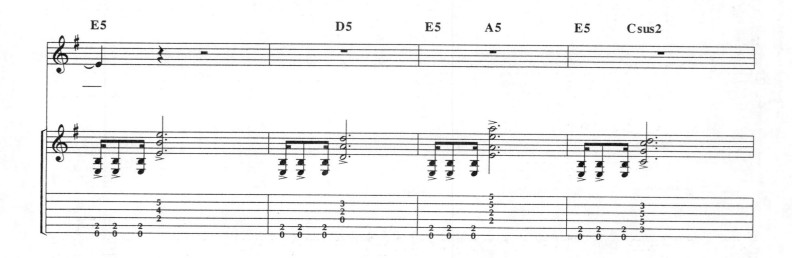

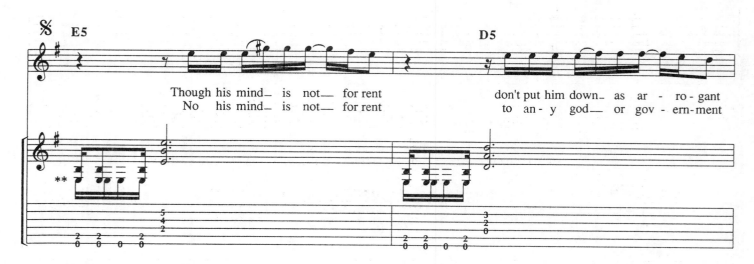

Though his mind— is not— for rent
No his mind— is not— for rent

don't put him down— as ar-ro-gant
to an-y god— or gov-ern-ment

* Bass and flanged keyboard Intro.
**Downstemmed figure on repeat.

Tom Sawyer - 6 - 1

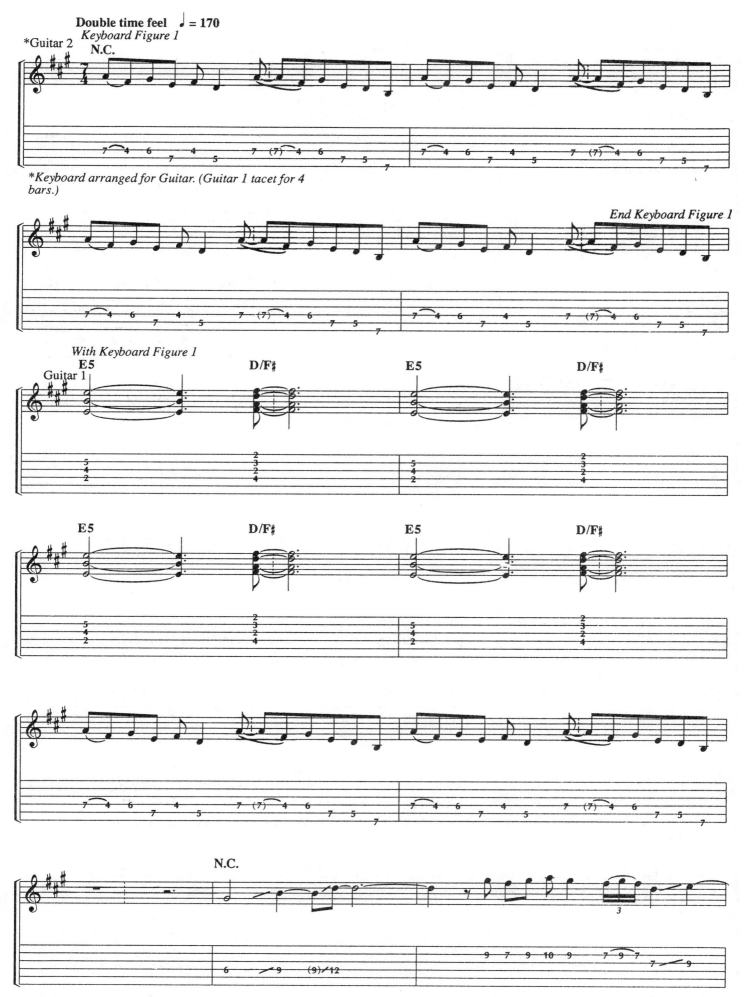

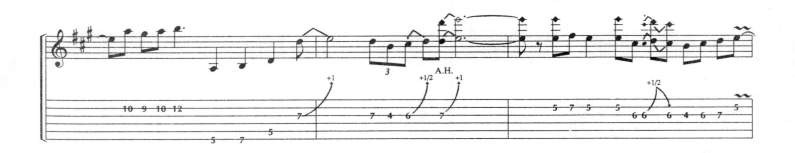

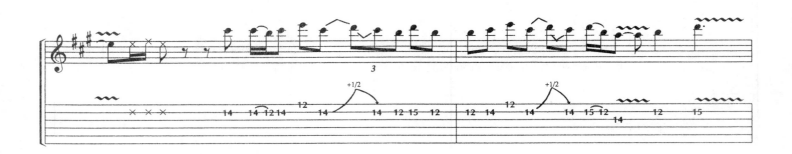

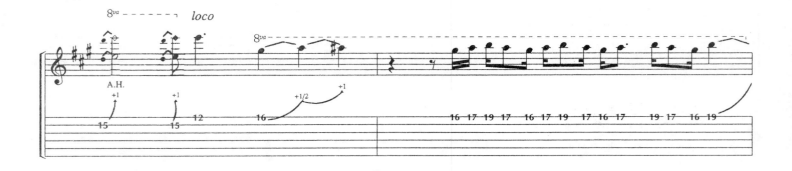

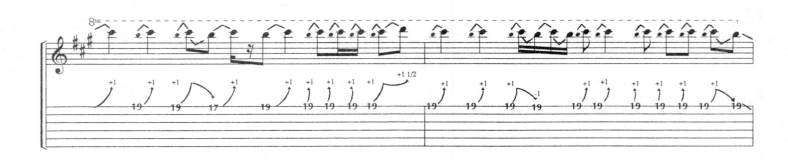

THE WARRIOR

Words and Music by
NICK GILDER and HOLLY KNIGHT

The Warrior - 6 - 1

w/Rhy. Fig. 3 *(Elec. Gtr. 3) 7 times, simile*
Cont. rhy. simile

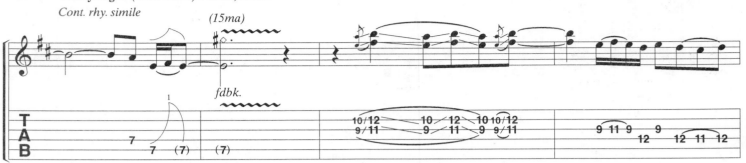

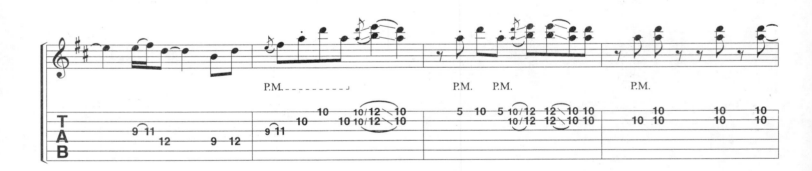

Chorus:

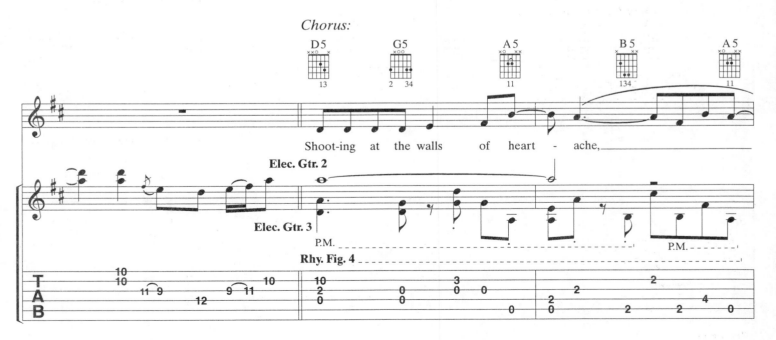

Shoot-ing at the walls of heart - ache,

Elec. Gtr. 2

Elec. Gtr. 3

Rhy. Fig. 4

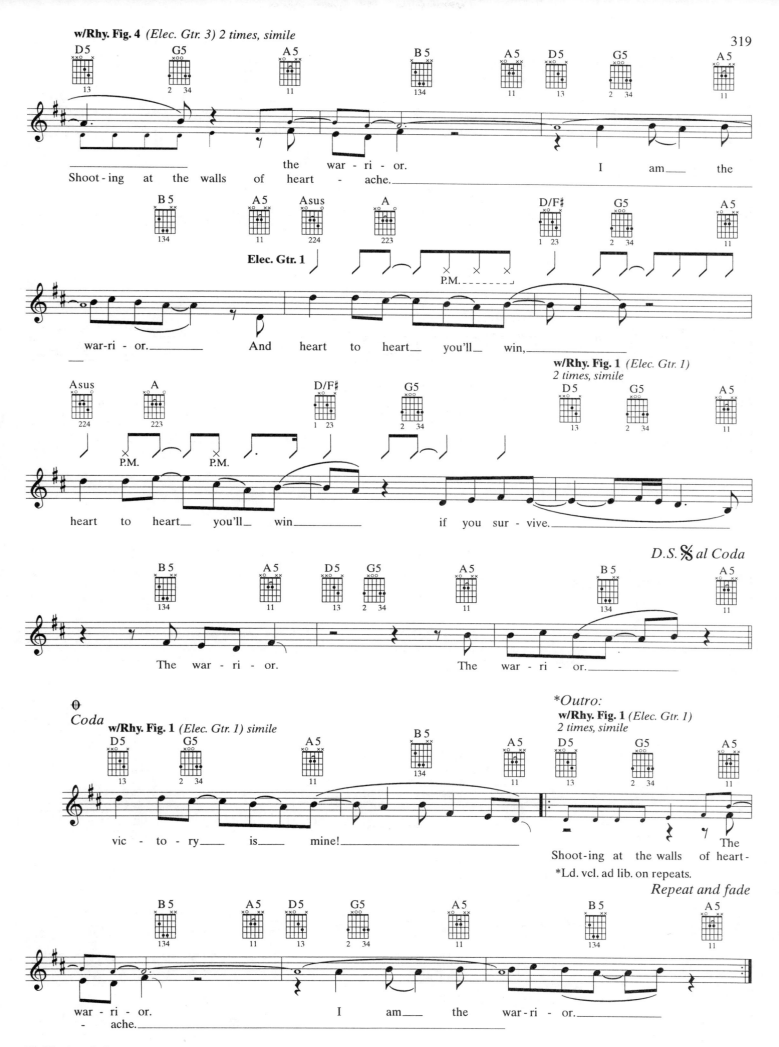

WHAT ABOUT LOVE

Words and Music by S. ALTON,
B. ALLEN and J. VALLANCE

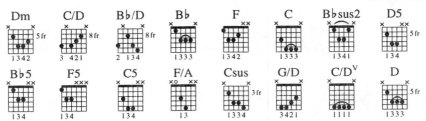

Moderately ♩ = 124

Intro:

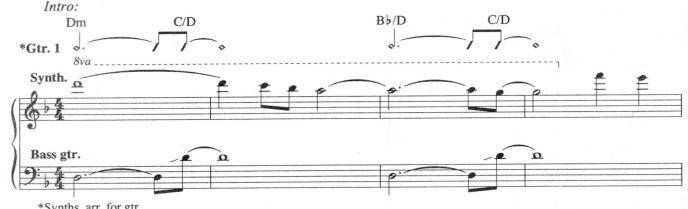

*Synths. arr. for gtr.

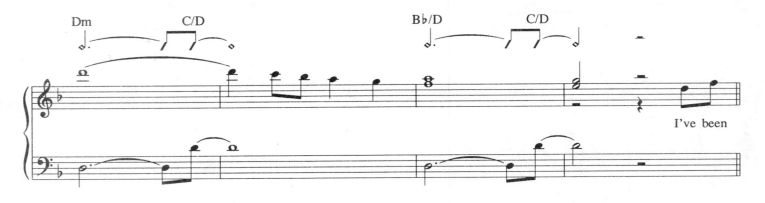

I've been

Verse 1:

lone - ly, I've been wait - ing for you. ___ I'm pre - tend - ing, and that's

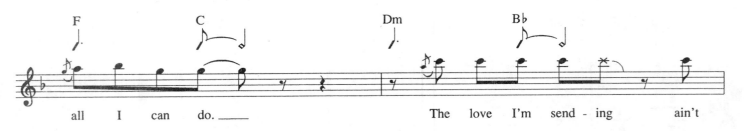

all I can do. ___ The love I'm send - ing ain't

What About Love - 5 - 1

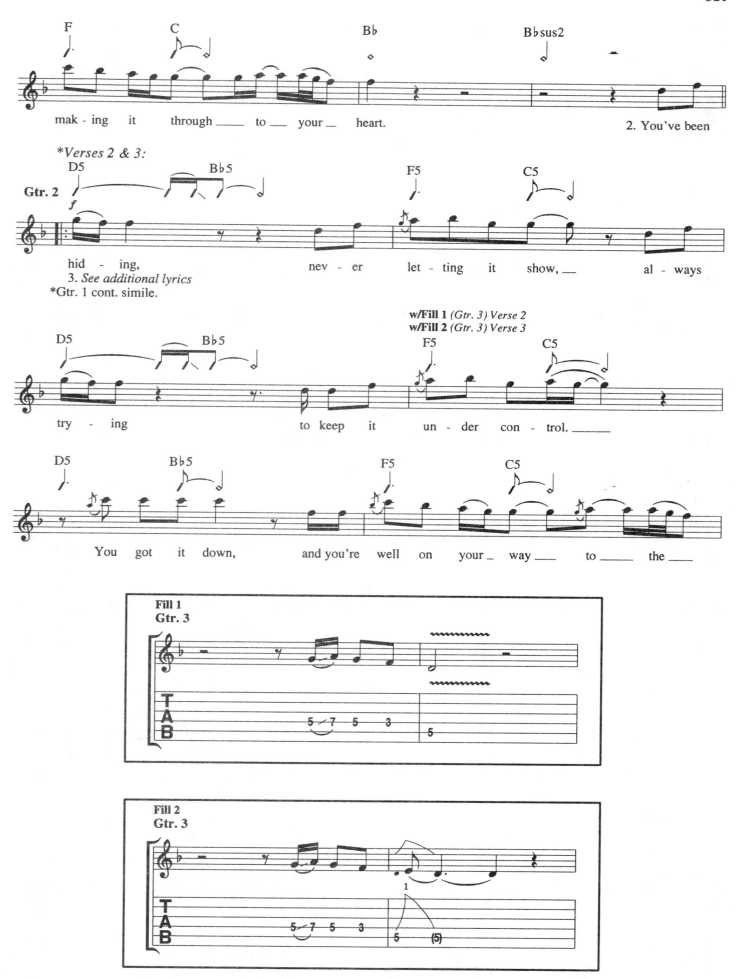

322

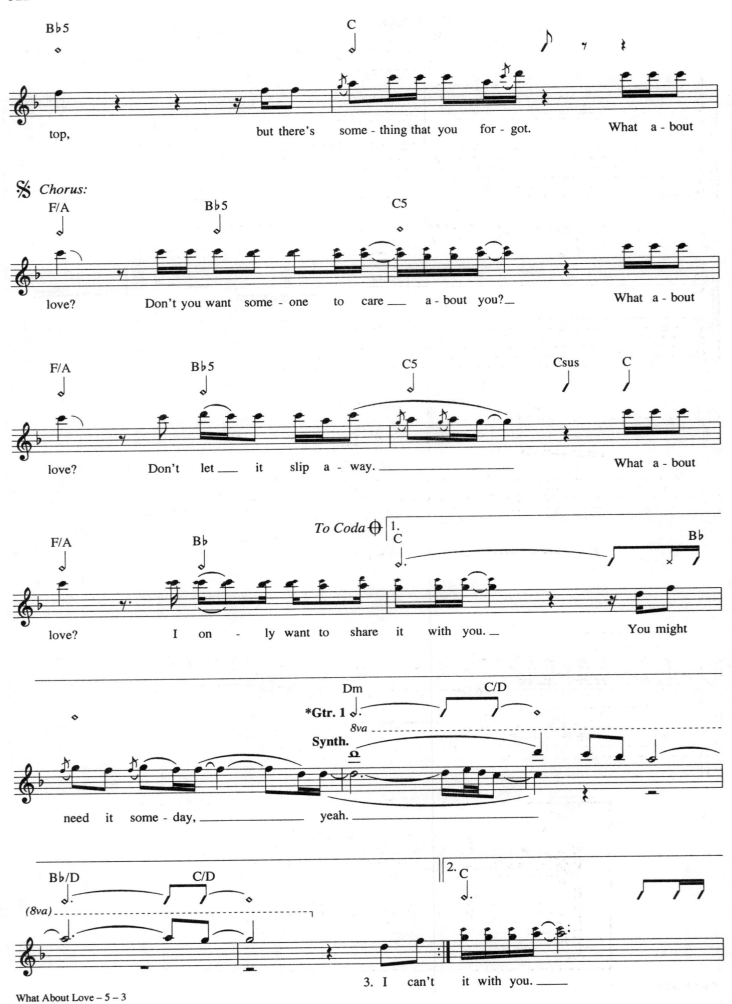

What About Love – 5 – 3

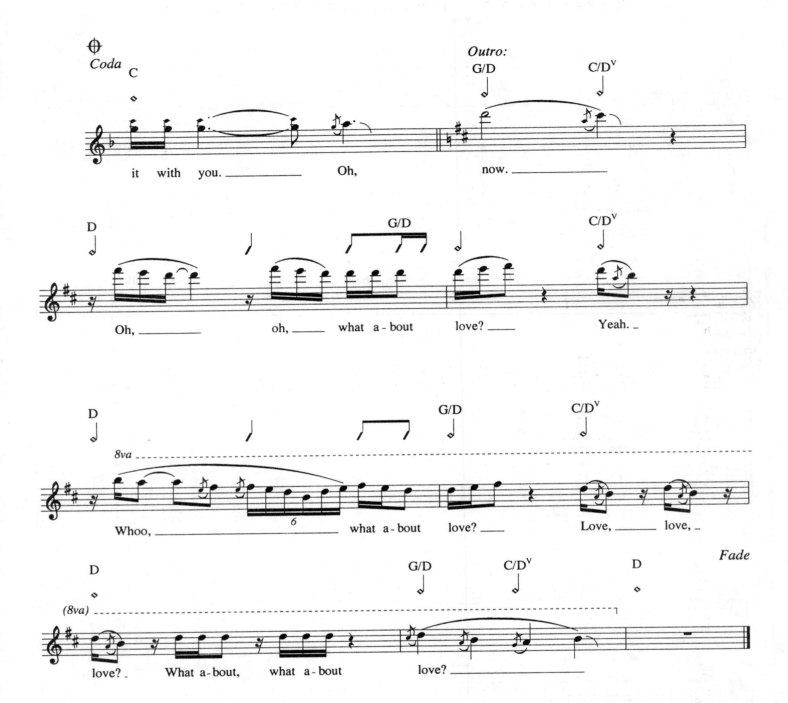

Verse 2:
I can't tell you what you're feeling inside.
And I can't sell you what you don't want to buy.
Something's missing; you gotta look back on your life.
You know something here just ain't right.
(To Chorus:)

YOU GIVE LOVE A BAD NAME

Words and Music by
JON BON JOVI, RICHIE SAMBORA
and DESMOND CHILD

You Give Love a Bad Name - 5 - 1

Verse

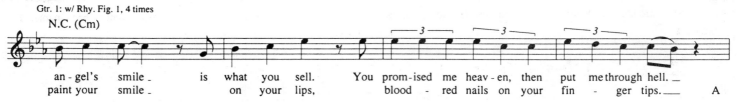

an - gel's smile __ is what you sell. You prom-ised me heav - en, then put me through hell.
paint your smile __ on your lips, blood - red nails on your fin - ger tips. __ A

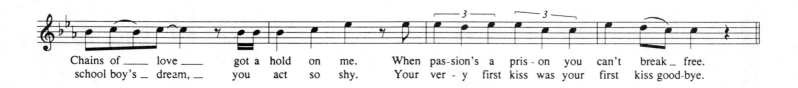

Chains of __ love __ got a hold on me. When pas-sion's a pris - on you can't break __ free.
school boy's __ dream, __ you act so shy. Your ver - y first kiss was your first kiss good-bye.

Pre-Chorus

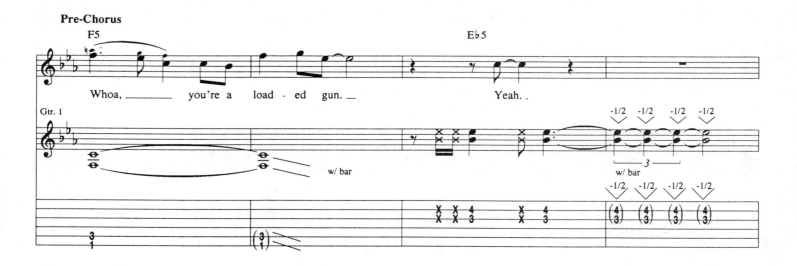

Whoa, _____ you're a load - ed gun. __ Yeah. __

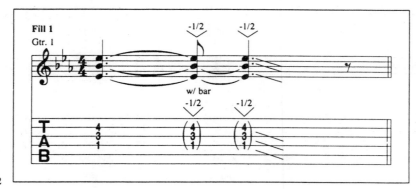

Fill 1
Gtr. 1

You Give Love a Bad Name - 5 - 3

* w/ harmonizer

328

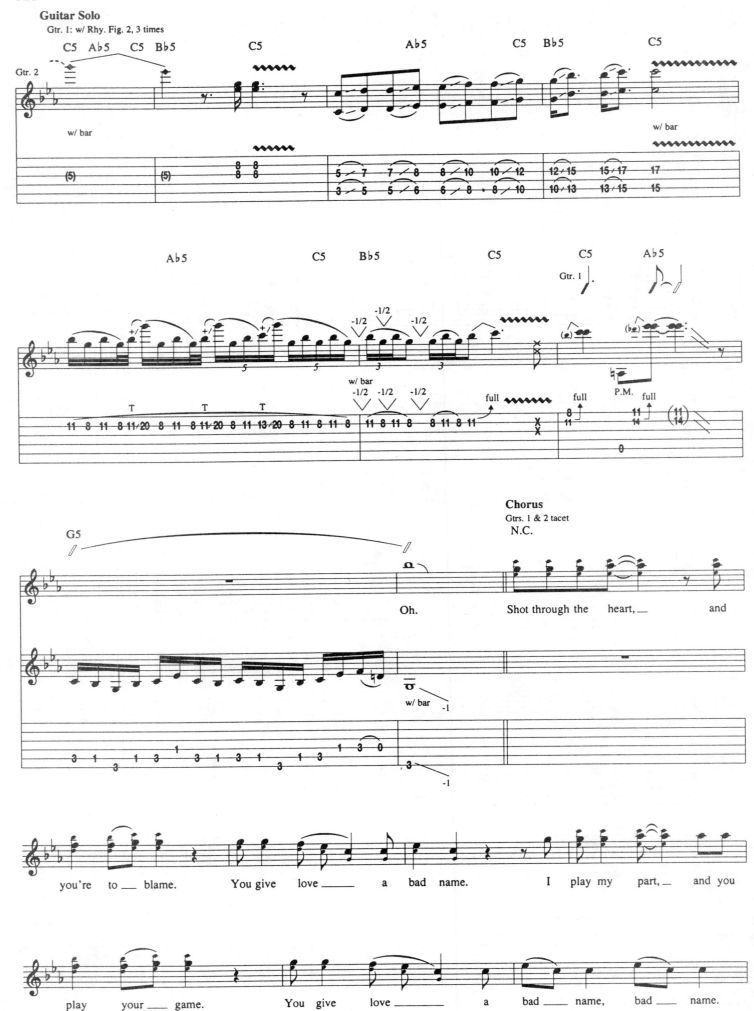

You Give Love a Bad Name - 5 - 4

*w/ harmonizer

WHITE WEDDING (Part 1)

Words and Music by
BILLY IDOL

White Wedding - 6 - 1

332

Interlude:

Take me back home, yeah!

GUITAR TAB GLOSSARY **

TABLATURE EXPLANATION

READING TABLATURE: Tablature illustrates the six strings of the guitar. Notes and chords are indicated by the placement of fret numbers on a given string(s).

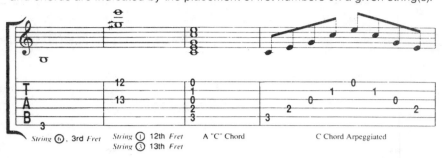

String ⑥, 3rd Fret   *String ① 12th Fret*   *A "C" Chord*   *C Chord Arpeggiated*
String ③ 13th Fret

BENDING NOTES

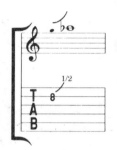

HALF STEP: Play the note and bend string one half step.*

WHOLE STEP: Play the note and bend string one whole step.

PREBEND AND RELEASE: Bend the string, play it, then release to the original note.

RHYTHM SLASHES

STRUM INDICA-TIONS: Strum with indicated rhythm.

The chord voicings are found on the first page of the transcription underneath the song title.

INDICATING SINGLE NOTES USING RHYTHM SLASHES: Very often single notes are incorporated into a rhythm part. The note name is indicated above the rhythm slash with a fret number and a string indication.

*A half step is the smallest interval in Western music; it is equal to one fret. A whole step equals two frets.

**By Kenn Chipkin and Aaron Stang

ARTICULATIONS

HAMMER ON: Play lower note, then "hammer on" to higher note with another finger. Only the first note is attacked.

PULL OFF: Play higher note, then "pull off" to lower note with another finger. Only the first note is attacked.

LEGATO SLIDE: Play note and slide to the following note. (Only first note is attacked).

PALM MUTE: The note or notes are muted by the palm of the pick hand by lightly touching the string(s) near the bridge.

ACCENT: Notes or chords are to be played with added emphasis.

DOWN STROKES AND UPSTROKES: Notes or chords are to be played with either a downstroke (⊓ ·) or upstroke (∨) of the pick.

© 1990 Beam Me Up Music
c/o CPP/Belwin, Inc. Miami, Florida 33014
International Copyright Secured   Made in U.S.A.   All Rights Reserved